praise for blissful bite.

"Christy Morgan's deliciously divine cookbook will help you heal and soar, one blissful bite at a time."
— Kris Carr, *New York Times* bestselling author

"Christy Morgan's beautiful cookbook is so much more than a collection of recipes. Time-saving food preparation tips, helpful cooking techniques, and kitchen tool recommendations are peppered among recipes that nourish the body, mind, and spirit. Blissful Bites *is a wonderful guide for those who want to experience the bliss of a plant-based diet!"*
— Colleen Patrick-Goudreau, bestselling author of such books as *The Joy of Vegan Baking*, *Color Me Vegan*, and *The 30-Day Vegan Challenge*

"Blissful Bites *is everything you've wanted on your path to optimal health, all in one beautiful book! The recipes are a paradise for your taste buds and a treat for your body. Christy Morgan has devised each one to bring you to the best of health in the most delicious possible way. If you want to slim down and boost your energy, or if you have any health concern—excess weight, high cholesterol, or diabetes, for example—this book will give you the tools you need. Christy Morgan's wonderful book makes the journey to health wonderfully easy and delicious!"*
— Neal Barnard, M.D., president, Physicians Committee for Responsible Medicine

"Finally—a cookbook that speaks directly to the soul! Christy Morgan's Blissful Bites *is a perfect combination of healthy and satisfying recipe ideas, both light and filling, with just the right mix of food philosophy and spiritual inspiration blended in. Emphasizing local, organic, seasonal, plant-based cuisine, there is a solid and friendly feel to this book that inspires trust and confidence. Highly recommended!"*
— Dr. Will Tuttle, Ph.D., author of the bestselling book *The World Peace Diet*, recipient of the *Courage of Conscience Award*, the co-founder of Circle of Compassion, and an acclaimed pianist and composer

"Blissful Bites *will take you on a spiritual culinary journey. It is filled with mouth-watering recipes that are healthy and easy to prepare. This cookbook should be a staple in everyone's kitchen."*
— Kim Barnouin, co-author of the #1 *New York Times* bestseller *Skinny Bitch*

"Blissful Bites *will inspire you to make delicious, healthy meals you'll enjoy feeding your family. Christy Morgan makes plant-based eating easy and addictive!"*
— Rory Freedman, co-author of the #1 *New York Times* bestseller *Skinny Bitch*

"I met Christy a couple of years ago and was struck immediately by her passion for good food and healthy living. Her energetic style shines in the pages of this book along with a depth of knowledge not often seen in such a young chef. I love this book: the variety, the options, the way she aligns—in harmony—

differing views on healthy eating. She blends macrobiotics, veganism, raw foods, and low-oil cooking to create truly blissful bites. A must-have for anyone interesting in healthy ... and blissful living."
— Christina Pirello, Emmy Award-winning host of the national public television series *Christina Cooks*, bestselling author of six books, including *Cooking the Whole Foods Way*, named "Healthiest Cookbook of the Decade" in January 2010

"The words 'clean,' 'wholesome,' and 'pure' spring off the page from this refreshing cookbook full of light, enticing recipes that put the 'being' back into 'human being.' You'll want to embrace the energy of whole foods and real meals made easy as pie with Blissful Bites.*"*
— Ingrid Newkirk, PETA founder

"What makes Christy's book, Blissful Bites: Vegan Meals That Nourish Mind, Body, and Planet, *stand out is her helpful nature, depth of knowledge, and ability to convey information to cooks of all skill levels in an enthusiastic, clear, and welcoming way. This book is a must-have for anyone's kitchen—vegan, macrobiotic, or just curious about eating healthy and delicious food."*
— Fran Costigan, author of *More Great Good Dairy Free Desserts Naturally*

"Using only healthy, whole food ingredients, Blissful Bites *is packed full of simple vegan recipes to help you add a delicious twist to any meal. This book is a must-have for every kitchen."*
— Ani Phyo, author of *Ani's Raw Food Asia*

"I am constantly amazed by Christy's ability to whip up stellar dishes seemingly out of thin air; she is prolific, talented, and an inspiration. Blissful Bites *is a must-have in any healthy kitchen."*
— Jessica Porter, author of *The Hip Chick's Guide to Macrobiotics*

Blissful Bites

Dedicated to everyone on a path to bliss

Blissful Bites

Vegan Meals That Nourish Mind, Body, and Planet

by Christy Morgan

The Blissful Chef

BenBella Books
Dallas, Texas

BenBella Books, Inc.
10300 N. Central Expressway, Suite 400
Dallas, TX 75231
www.benbellabooks.com
Send feedback to feedback@benbellabooks.com

Printed in the United States of America
10 9 8 7 6 5 4 3 2 1

Library of Congress Cataloging-in-Publication Data is available for this title.
ISBN: 978-1-935618-51-5

Editing by Debbie Harmsen and Sara Cassidy
Copyediting by Sherri Lerner
Proofreading by Stacia Seaman
Cover design by Kit Sweeney
Text design and composition by Kit Sweeney
Photographs by Melissa Schwartz and Melanie Shatto
www.schwartzstudios.com
www.melaniemorganshatto.com
Index by Christy Morgan
Printed by Bang Printing

Distributed by Perseus Distribution
www.perseusdistribution.com

To place orders through Perseus Distribution:
Tel: 800-343-4499
Fax: 800-351-5073

E-mail: orderentry@perseusbooks.com

table of contents

first things first

the recipes

more

chef favorites

breakfast and brunch of champions • coconut bliss granola (page 35)
appetizers and soups for every occasion • asian rice paper rolls (page 81)
salads • zucchini "pasta" with mint-cashew pesto sauce (page 92)
delectable vegetable sides • lemon-kissed brussels and butternut squash (page 119)
whole grains and carbs do a body good • sushi rice bowl (page 148)
sea vegetables • soba noodle sushi with apricot-ginger dipping sauce (page 170)
compassionate proteins • un-tuna salad (page 206)
healthier desserts you crave • gluten-free peanut butter cookies (page 226)

fan favorites

breakfast and brunch of champions • pineapple cornbread muffins (page 37)
appetizers and soups for every occasion • lemony-lime hummus (page 60)
salads • spring kale salad with sweet miso dressing (page 88)
delectable vegetable sides • magical raw tacos (page 114)
whole grains and carbs do a body good • macro "mac and cheeze" (page 150)
sea vegetables • land and sea soba salad (page 169)
compassionate proteins • curry chicken-less salad (page 187)
healthier desserts you crave • heavenly raw chocolate mousse (page 220)

foreword

I love food. Actually, I am downright crazy about it. But I also love to feel healthy. Sometimes the two can create a tough balance ... especially as a vegan.

A decade ago, I was living on junk and fast foods. Even though I enjoyed every bite, the reality of eating that junk for so many years began to catch up with me. I couldn't figure out why I was constantly feeling like crap. So I started to explore the possible causes, and finally some research on my health issues led me to the disturbing finding that these ailments might be a product of what I was eating. It all became clear when I discovered the concept of healing through food. I thought it sounded crazy at first, but I decided to give it a try. After all, what did I have to lose? To my amazement, I started to get better. Then I started to feel better than I had in years, all thanks to food—the right food, that is. After about a year of refining my diet, I decided to study holistic nutrition and share what worked for me with anyone who would listen. The light bulb went off in my head and my mission was born: Help as many people as possible change the way they eat. Thus, the *Skinny Bitch* series was born.

I first met Christy in late summer of 2009 for a blind "lunch date" at Seed Café in Venice Beach, California. We both knew prior to the lunch that we had a lot in common. We're both crazy about food and passionate about helping people get healthy. In getting to know Christy, I learned about the path that brought her to where she is today and how her own discoveries of the healing powers of foods led her to be a powerhouse in the kitchen and a true educator through her cooking classes, instructional videos, and role as a blogger. I became one of the fortunate who have experienced first-hand just how amazing her dishes are, after she came to my house and worked her magic in my kitchen. (Note to parents reading this book: even my then 3-year-old son loved every bite.)

Christy has an immense knowledge of good food and the health benefits it provides the body. This cookbook—sure to set your mouth watering—proves that when knowledge is paired with tried and true experience in the kitchen, the results are dishes that not only taste amazing, but are some of the healthiest recipes on the block.

In this cookbook, Christy takes you by the hand and eases you into her world by teaching you how to stock your pantry and the best kitchenware for your needs, how to cook in sync with the seasons, and integrate fresh, natural, unprocessed and unrefined foods into every meal. These elements, as Christy explains, are responsible for the nourishment of your mind, body, and spirit.

Who knew that healthy eating could taste so delicious! Diving into the world of vegan cooking may seem daunting at first, but Christy's passion for bringing this cuisine into everyone's kitchen makes it seem like a breeze.

I often hear people complain that they simply don't have much time to cook. They also have this idea that cooking a plant-based diet is too time-consuming. The reality is that it's no different than cooking any other kind of food—it just takes some preparation in the beginning and an open mind. Let Christy guide you through the wonderful world of plant-based cooking, and you will reap all of the benefits it has to offer. You might just find it was the lifestyle you've been looking for all along.

—Kim Barnouin, co-author of *Skinny Bitch*

"Follow your bliss and the universe will open doors where there were only walls."

— Joseph Campbell

first things first

finding your bliss

Can eating healthy lead us to bliss?

To feel bliss is to experience great happiness or spiritual joy. If our diets are filled with junk, we don't feel vibrant, sexy, and alive–we aren't experiencing true bliss. What we eat has a powerful and profound effect on our entire life. The food that we take in becomes every cell in our body, making up our physical, psychological, and spiritual health. Who knew that such a simple act, which we do at least three times a day, is possibly *the* answer to all our problems?

Our health is in a state of crisis. It continues to decline as we are bombarded with fad diets and advertisements for the next quick fix. Our food is sprayed with chemicals and genetically modified; corporations don't look out for our best interests; and cheap, unhealthy fast food continues to be more affordable than healthful meals that nourish us. Since you were drawn to this book, you are probably seeking a change.

Maybe you feel disconnected from your friends, coworkers, and family. Maybe you don't have enough energy to play with your kids. Or perhaps you are sick of the diet rollercoaster and are ready to get off and try something more effective. Do you feel blissful on a daily basis? When you wake up in the morning, do you jump out of bed feeling energetic and ready for anything? If not, then it's time to make a change!

Eating seasonal, local, plant-based foods is the key. The nutrient-rich dishes made from such foods can help you feel radiant, alive, and in tune with your body as well as with the surrounding environment. In a phrase: It lets you find your bliss.

What is bliss? Bliss is being so comfortable in your own skin that you feel tapped into the greater universe. I know it sounds trippy, but hear me out.

After years of study, I have found my bliss. On a daily basis I experience deep contentment. It's my hope that in sharing this message with you, I'll introduce you to the best food you've ever tasted, while connecting you to the greater scheme of life. Through this cookbook, let me take you on a culinary journey that will enlighten your taste buds and put some pep in your step.

I'm not a traditional chef. I didn't go to a traditional culinary school. My focus is on your health. The food you'll find in this cookbook is real food—meaning it is in its natural state, pure and simple, unadulterated and completely whole. The dishes here complement a mix of

vegan and flexitarian

*You've probably heard the word **vegetarian**; it means a diet that excludes animal meats. The vegan diet expands its view of animals by cutting out all animal products, including dairy, eggs, and even honey. Most vegans also do not wear clothing, shoes, and accessories made from animals or buy products that were tested on animals.*

*Donald Watson came up with the word **vegan** in 1944 by combining the first three and last two letters of **vegetarian**. Today, a new term, **flexitarian**, is used to describe someone who eats mostly vegetarian meals but still eats animal foods on occasion—they haven't made the full jump to vegetarianism or veganism.*

If that's you, that's okay. You aren't being judged here. I just want you to dip your toe in and feel your bliss start to skyrocket. What I have found is that when I eat a sustainable, plant-based diet I can connect to my bliss. That means I eat an array of plant foods in balance with my surrounding environment that can truly nourish me.

traditional plant-based diets—vegetarian, vegan, macrobiotic, low-fat, and raw foods—so whichever diet you follow (or are ready to start following), you'll be able to whip up dozens of dishes to suit your needs. What you won't find in these pages is chemical-laden, preservative-filled fake food. This cookbook has recipes that support your health while never leaving you feeling deprived.

Seek guidance from your doctor when starting a new eating plan, but remember—you know your body better than anyone. Trust your intuition. Switching to a plant-based diet may feel strange at first. Some people will be able to eliminate animal foods and processed sugary foods all together. But if that is too difficult for you, start by adding more whole grains and green leafy vegetables to your meals, making the transition gradually.

If you eat a diet rich in whole grains, legumes, fruits, vegetables, nuts, and seeds, you can greatly enhance the disease-resisting abilities of your body.

As you start to transform your diet and health, you'll begin to see the bigger picture staring back at you from your dinner plate: you will look at food as fuel for your body and mind, not something purely to satisfy a sensory craving.

The food in this cookbook will take you on a journey toward bliss. Every recipe in this cookbook is plant-based and vegan, meaning there is absolutely no call for animal products. So not only does this diet improve your health and happiness, but it helps you be kind to our animal friends, too.

a plant-based diet

This isn't a book about dieting. I don't like the word *diet* that is associated with restricted calories and negative thoughts about ourselves. You may have tried a few of these diets but gained the weight back and felt defeated. The only way to lose weight and keep it off is to change your eating habits and lifestyle for good. If one of your goals is to lose weight, yet not sacrifice taste or joy, this cookbook will make that easier, because eating a whole-food, plant-based diet can help you lose weight in a way that enhances your overall health.

Maybe you don't need to lose weight and you don't have a serious health condition. You can still

blissful tip: the good, better, best policy

Moderation is key when transitioning to a plant-based diet. A teacher of mine taught me to use the "good, better, best" policy when it comes to choosing food. Ask yourself, "Is this the best choice I have at the moment?"

Choose minimally processed and less packaged food. Processed food is junk that contains little nutritional value and is usually high in fat with poor-quality salt and sugar. It's not real food. More energy goes into producing this food than what it actually provides, and the waste from the packaging produces more trash to haul to the landfills, wasting precious resources simply for our convenience of a packaged meal. (Don't even get me started on individually wrapped junk food!)

If your local grocery store has bulk bins, check those out for snack food. You can bring a reusable bag and load up on nuts, dried fruit, granola, sesame sticks, and whatever else is available. Or you can have an apple instead of packaged food. Eating fruit creates very little waste, and the waste it does make is biodegradable.

blissful trick: When you go grocery shopping, stick to the perimeter or outside aisles of the store. The junk food tends to be on the inside aisles.

items to be reduced or avoided

When using the "good, better, best" policy, there are some foods that would be good to limit because they are harsh on our organs and damaging to our mental state. These include meat, dairy, eggs, alcohol, caffeine, and junk food with additives and hydrogenated oil. Sugar and alcohol demineralize the body, weakening the immune system, which causes deficiencies and overly acidic blood. If you continue to eat sugar and drink alcohol after giving up animal foods, you will not reap the complete benefits of a healthy plant-based diet. Remember, it's not just about the food you put in your mouth, but rather about embodying a holistic lifestyle that supports and nourishes you in every way.

benefit from the principles in this book, because prevention is the best medicine. If you eat a diet rich in whole grains, legumes, fruits, vegetables, nuts, and seeds, you can greatly enhance the disease-resisting abilities of your body. If your heart is healthy and your immune system is strong, you will have a decreased incidence of the common cold, flu, headaches, allergies, and even such conditions as cancer, heart disease, asthma, arthritis, and diabetes—as well as almost every other disease affecting us today.

The benefits of switching to a plant-based diet are immense, almost immeasurable. Wonderful things happen for nearly everyone who takes the plunge: clear and radiant skin, weight loss, more energy, better sleep, better sex, less stress and anxiety, better digestion, and the greatest gift of all, feeling a deeper connection to the world around you. Eating this way does less harm to the earth than a meat-centered diet that uses precious water, land, and resources. Are you open to the idea that your diet can influence every ounce of your existence?

Eating a plant-based diet is what sets you down a path of bliss. But let's take our plant-based diet a step further by eating local, seasonal, organic foods when possible. With local farmers markets, natural food stores, and online suppliers just a click away, it's never been easier to eat a healthy, organic vegan diet.

the marvels of macrobiotics

Along my path to bliss, I studied macrobiotics as part of my holistic nutrition training. Macrobiotics is about creating balance in your body, on your plate, and in your mind and heart. It's about eating whole foods and knowing what your body wants and needs. Studying macrobiotic principles gave me a foundation for optimal health that I couldn't experience just by being vegan. In fact, because a macrobiotic diet is known to improve overall health, many people with chronic illnesses turn to this way of eating.

The macrobiotic diet is not a one-size-fits-all regimen. By practicing a macrobiotic lifestyle,

a word about the allium family

One thing that you'll notice in this cookbook is that most of the recipes do not include members of the garlic or onion family, or when they do, that it's an optional ingredient. If you are already vegetarian or vegan, consider decreasing the onion and garlic family (scallions, leeks, shallots, chives, etc.) in your diet. This will help you feel lighter and more energetic. Garlic is a medicinal herb used to kill bacteria and is not like the food-grade herbs that can be taken daily or in larger amounts. If you eat a plant-based diet, eating onion and garlic is like taking antibiotics when you don't need it. Onions and garlic also are known to have heavy energy, or qi, that can weigh you down and be taxing on your digestive system. Why would you want to eat something that makes you cry like a baby when you chop it, makes your breath and body smell funky, and makes you pass gas? This is your body telling you to stop eating it, so listen more closely to its message. If you look at many Eastern spiritual traditions, onion and garlic are excluded from the diet because it stimulates passion, lust, anxiety, and rage. It's hard to feel bliss and think clearly if you are consumed by all these emotions.

This change may be a hard challenge for many, because onion and garlic have become staples of the American diet, especially the vegetarian, vegan, and macrobiotic diets. You are more than welcome to add onions and garlic to any recipe in this book, but I encourage you to try as an experiment for a week to go sans allium family to see the difference in how you feel. It will be hard to avoid onion and garlic if you eat packaged foods or at restaurants often, but it *is* possible to reduce the amount you are consuming, and to eliminate it completely from your own cooking. Read food labels at the grocery store, and when ordering food at restaurants, ask the waiter or chef what is best to order, or just ask that the onion and garlic be left out of your meal.

you have the freedom to make conscious decisions for your individual mind, body, and spirit. But first you have to get clean to be able to hear the right messages.

What I mean by "clean" is to give up sugar, coffee, simple carbs (such as white bread, pasta, and processed foods, alcohol, animal foods, and other unnecessary items) anywhere from three to six months. This will allow your body to discharge and detox the junk that has been

> Whether you are on a budget, need to lose weight, have a busy life, or need to heal from an illness or injury, this cookbook and its teachings will help you get back in balance.

stored up from eating a meat-centered diet. During this time, substitute those subtracted things with natural, organic, plant-based, whole foods. Most likely after your detox period you won't want to add the not-so-clean stuff back into your diet because you'll be feeling so good!

You will be amazed at the difference in how you feel on this lighter diet. You will feel healthier and begin to understand what your body wants and needs. A little bit of bliss will call out to you, urging you to continue down a path that makes you feel good.

Whether you are on a budget, need to lose weight, have a busy life, or need to heal from an illness or injury, this cookbook and its teachings can help you get back in balance. The cookbook combines philosophies that I have found to work—for myself, and for countless other people. It can give you the freedom to make conscious decisions that allow you to nourish yourself and help you connect to your bliss.

how to read this cookbook

There is something for everyone in this book, whether you are vegetarian, vegan, eating mostly raw foods, or trying to stay clear of gluten, soy, or oil. Almost all the recipes are gluten-free by default, and most of them use hardly any oil, if at all. Icons next to a recipe indicate whether it has low or no oil, is gluten-free, soy-free, and/or raw, and if it takes less than 45 minutes to prepare. Sprinkled throughout the book are tips on living a sustainable and blissful existence that transcends your diet.

As the seasons change, the produce that is available locally changes as well. If we take our cues from nature regarding what foods we should eat during each season, we can take pleasure in the bounty Mother Nature provides. Throughout this book, keep a lookout for different font colors to signify each recipe's season. Keeping order

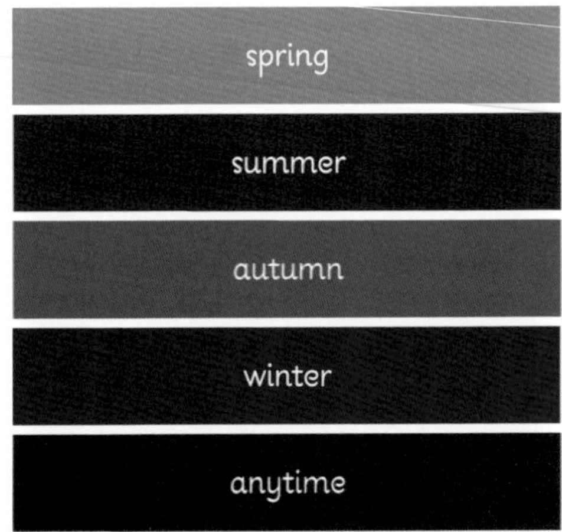

with the earthly seasons, the recipes flow from spring (green), to summer (maroon), to autumn (orange), and finally to winter (blue). After winter, because some recipes are pretty neutral, I have also provided you with an "anytime" section (brown).

Eating seasonally with produce grown in your region is not only the best way to be in balance with your surrounding environment, but it also lessens our dependence on fossil fuels. Your food isn't traveling long distances to get on your plate—making it the freshest it can be and friendly to the environment. You aren't contributing to the carbon crisis, which should make you feel a little warm and fuzzy inside.

I'm not saying you have to give up those delicious tropical fruits like coconuts and mangoes completely. You'll even find some of them in this book. But think about the traveling they do, when they are out of season, to get to your grocery store. We can always make little changes to our daily diets to help nourish the planet.

the icons

RAW • If your diet is predominantly raw or living foods, you're in for a treat, as there are many recipes in this cookbook just for you. If it's warm outside or you just need some freshness in your life, look for the recipes with this symbol.

GLUTEN-FREE • If you have an allergy or sensitivity to gluten, look for recipes with this symbol.

SOY-FREE • It is possible to eat plant-based if you are trying to avoid soy. Granted, not all soy is created equal, but if you are allergic to soy sauce, tempeh, tofu, edamame, miso, or any other soy-derived product, you'll want to look for the recipes with this symbol.

LOW OR NO OIL • At least half the recipes in this book contain no oil and the others almost all contain less than a tablespoon of oil. Oil is optional in the recipes that call for it, so you can leave it out of most recipes if you are watching your oil intake.

LESS THAN 45 MINUTES • My recipes are loved because they are simple yet delicious. Some take longer than others, though, so if you are looking for a quick meal that can be ready in under 45 minutes, including prep time, look for recipes with this symbol.

CHEF FAVORITE • Since these are my delicious recipes, I took it upon myself to notify you of my personal favorites.

FAN FAVORITE • My friends, clients, and recipe testers love all my recipes, but I've asked them to tell me which ones are their favorites. The recipes that an overwhelming number of people like are marked by this icon.

Now that you know what the icons and the colors represent, I will help you create the ideal kitchen space with an equipment list of essential cookware, a pantry basics list so you know what to buy for your blissful kitchen, and prepping tips to make cooking easier and faster. After you accomplish those steps you will be on your way to making blissful meals and feeling great!

creating the ideal kitchen space and pantry

Knowing how to stock your pantry, set up your kitchen cabinets, and organize your tools can be a lifesaver. If you keep a well-stocked pantry with a variety of whole grains, nuts, seeds, proteins, spices, and herbs, you are less likely to eat out or reach for junk food. A few of the ingredients found in this cookbook may be unfamiliar or unusual to you, though most can be found at any grocery store. I try to use the highest-quality foods available in my cooking, and I hope you'll experiment with healthy alternatives. Unusual items will be available at any natural food store, but I've listed some websites in the resources section in the back of the book where you can find them as well. If there is something you can't find, you can substitute a similar item. If you have questions about substituting, please contact me via my website (*theblissfulchef.com*), and I can offer suggestions. Below are my favorite pantry items that I have stocked at all times.

pantry basics

spices

These are the dried spices I most commonly use.

- basil
- bay leaves
- black pepper
- caraway
- cayenne
- celery seed
- chili powder
- cinnamon
- coriander
- cumin, whole and ground
- curry powder
- dill weed
- fennel seeds
- garam masala
- ginger
- marjoram
- mint
- nutmeg
- oregano
- paprika
- parsley
- rosemary
- sage
- tarragon
- thyme
- turmeric
- white pepper

blissful suggestion

Buy spices in bulk at the local co-op. Buying organic spices in containers costs more than double what you would pay for bulk because you are paying for the glass container as well. I like to buy spices in a bottle and then refill the bottle with spices bought in bulk. That way I am buying only the small amount that I need, ensuring that my spices are as fresh as they can be.

oils, vinegars, condiments, and seasonings

Along with spices, there are other pantry basics that I always have on hand to cook with. It isn't required to have all these things, but I like to have options so I never get bored.

vinegars	oils	condiments	salt/seasonings
apple cider	coconut	dijon mustard	barley miso
balsamic	flax and hemp	nutritional yeast	coconut aminos
brown rice	grapeseed	sauerkraut	himalayan pink salt
red wine	olive	stone-ground mustard	sea salt
sherry	safflower	unsweetened ketchup	shoyu (soy sauce)
umeboshi	toasted sesame	vegan worcester sauce	tamari
	walnut	vegenaise or vegan mayonnaise	white miso

baking stuff

Everyone loves to bake—or at least loves things baked for them! These are my essential pantry ingredients for baking, including my preferred sweeteners and flours.

flour	sweeteners	other essentials	flavoring/extracts
almond	amasake	almond milk	almond
barley	barley malt	applesauce	lemon
brown rice	brown rice syrup	arrowroot	mint
garbanzo/fava	coconut palm sugar	baking powder	orange
kamut	dates	baking soda	vanilla
unbleached white	fruit jams	flax meal	
wheat pastry	maple syrup	nut butters	

other staples

I keep my kitchen pantry filled with a variety of whole grains, beans, nuts, seeds, dried fruit, and healthy snacks so I'm never caught empty-handed when I need to whip up a meal.

the tools

To get the most out of your whole foods preparation, you'll want to outfit your kitchen with basic tools that will have you cooking blissful meals in no time. Having the right tools makes cooking enjoyable and saves you time and money in the long run. Some things are essential; some are optional. I've organized tools into these two categories below.

Quality is important. Think of your kitchen tools as a lifetime investment. If you spend the money now on good-quality tools, you won't have to spend more time or money later. Remember that more expensive doesn't necessarily mean better. Discount department stores, like Ross and Marshall's, for example, carry name-brand products at a discount, so start there.

Some brands are known for being tried and true. I've included some of my favorite brands in the equipment list on the following pages.

blissful suggestion

Throw out your microwave. It changes the molecular structure of the food and destroys some of its vital nutrients. You will find you're able to live without it sooner than you think. Let's start making fresh meals that nourish mind, body, and planet!

essential

quality knives

The most important things in your kitchen repertoire are good knives. In my knife collection, I have three knives: a chef knife that I use for almost everything, a paring knife for small jobs, and a bread or serrated knife for slicing bread or soft fruits like tomatoes. Those last two knives can be any brand really; save the dough for your main knife.

I like Global, NHS, and MAC knives. I have found these to be the most durable, easy-to-work-with and sharpest chef knives; they are priced around $70 to $125 apiece. The NHS is Japanese, made from the same high-carbon steel that samurai swords are made from, so you know it's one sharp mofo. Make sure they stay sharp, and be sure to tuck your fingers while you chop so no blood is shed. Having a good sharp knife makes cooking and prepping so much easier, faster, and more enjoyable than using a dull, bad slicer. Once you try a high-quality chef knife you will never go back!

After you get this marvelous knife, you need to take care of it properly. When you are finished with it, always wash it, dry it completely, and store it in its knife guard—never leave it sitting in the sink with food crusting on it. If you leave it sitting around, it will start to rust and dull. Also, never scrape the blade side of your knife along the cutting board like they all do on those Food Network shows (my biggest pet peeve ever!). This will dull your knife. However, you can use the backside to pick up chopped veggies. (Alternatively, use a dough scraper to sweep up those veggies.) I have my chef knives professionally sharpened only twice a year because I take good care of them.

wood or bamboo cutting board

For vegan cooking, get rid of your plastic cutting boards (save them for meat products, if using, and keep separate for safety). You want a nice thick bamboo cutting board. I prefer one that is at least 20x15 with a juice groove. Simply Bamboo and Totally Bamboo are great brands.

blissful trick

To keep your cutting board from slipping around, lightly dampen a paper towel or thin dish towel and place it underneath your cutting board.

colander and mesh strainer

One large stainless steel colander will do the trick for draining pasta and veggies. I have a variety of styles and sizes of mesh strainers for

left to right: bamboo utensil, Le Creuset spatula, Microplane zester, front: dough scraper, back: citrus reamer, mini mesh strainer, chef knife, paring knife

other jobs: a two-inch with a handle for catching seeds when juicing citrus, an eight-inch with a handle for sifting flour, an eight-inch stand-up for washing/straining grains, and a skimmer, which is essential for blanching vegetables.

food processor and blender

A good blender and food processor are essentials in a blissful kitchen. I could not survive without my Vitamix. The reason you need both is because the blender is for the more liquid things, like smoothies, dressings, pureed soups, etc., while the food processor is used for more chunky recipes that don't contain a lot of liquid, such as bean pâtés, pestos, etc. Processors also have cool attachments that help you grate and chop veggies if you are feeling too lazy to cut them by hand. Both of these are a lifetime investment and are worth every single penny.

Cuisinart is tried and true—just go for the bigger bowl at 11 or 14 inches. You will be fine with less expensive brands, too.

pots, pans, and casserole dishes

Throw out Teflon nonstick and aluminum pans. There are toxic chemicals found in the coating on these pans. Replace with stainless steel, cast iron, enamel-coated cast iron, or glass. There are many new "green" companies making nonstick pans that are purported to be nontoxic. I don't feel like there's enough research to know for sure if these pans are safe, but they are great to use when making pancakes or crêpes, for toasting nuts, and for things that benefit from a nonstick surface or low-oil cooking. Use your own judgment if you want to try these pans.

Essential pans are a small saucepan, large stockpot, and both large and small sauté/skillet/fry pan. You want to have lids that fit all these pans as well. For casserole dishes, get glass or ceramic/porcelain in a variety of sizes. Pyrex makes a variety of sets that can be your new best friend. You'll need a large one that's 13x9 inches, a two-quart one, and an 8x8 inch square dish.

pressure cooker

If you don't already have one, jump in and buy a pressure cooker. Cooking fresh beans will be a snap, and brown rice made in a pressure cooker is heaven on earth. One brand that is great and not expensive is Fagor. Or you can go fancier with Kuhn Rikon. Either way, I prefer them to rice cookers because they have more uses.

bamboo/wood and stainless steel utensils

Get a variety of utensils in varying sizes with long handles, like a spoon, slotted spoon, rice paddle, ladle, whisk, and tongs. Bamboo and stainless steel utensils are better than plastic ones. When you cook with plastic, the heat is melting the utensils and thus the material's particles are going into your food. Just be sure not to use the stainless steel utensils on any cookware that can be scratched. For that cookware, use bamboo or one of my favorite tools, the *Le Creuset* spatula. It can be heated up to 500 degrees F, making it a versatile tool to have in your healthy kitchen. I also like to have a pair of bamboo cooking chopsticks. They always come in handy.

stainless steel and glass bowls, dough scraper

I like to keep glass and stainless steel bowls of various sizes and a dough scraper by my prepping station. The scraper helps me quickly pick up chopped veggies and place them in a bowl to make room on the cutting board for the next chopping project.

measuring cups and spoons

Get glass (not plastic) liquid measuring cups, at least one four-cup and one two-cup; stainless steel dry measuring cups that usually come in a set; and a couple of sets of stainless steel measuring spoons.

steamer baskets and sushi mat

I like to have both the stainless steel steamer basket that opens up and the bamboo kind that has many layers. Sushi mats come in handy to make...well, sushi—but I also use them as space savers by covering a bowl with a mat, then putting another bowl on top and so on. This is great when soaking both grains and beans in separate bowls.

vegetable scrubbers, peelers, graters, citrus reamers

If your produce is organic, and I hope it is, you don't need to peel it. Just buy a vegetable scrub brush and scrub it under running water. But for the times that you do need a peeler, it's good to have a few on hand, both the usual straight kind and the Y-shaped. I find the kind you slip on one finger a bit awkward. As for graters, my favorite brand is Microplane, but the standard box variety will do just fine.

Fun tools to have in your repertoire are a Microplane zester and a citrus reamer. Adding citrus juice (e.g., lemon, lime, orange) and citrus zest is a lovely way to turn a regular recipe into something gourmet. Be sure to lightly zest the outside of the fruit, being careful not to zest into the white parts because that is bitter. You can use the zester to grate ginger as well to make ginger juice.

blissful trick

Store extra citrus zest or grated ginger in a small glass jar in the freezer for up to a month so you have it available for another recipe.

spray bottle

A spray bottle is great to have for putting oil in to make your own pan spray, instead of buying the aerosol stuff from the store. I like the stainless steel kind as opposed to the plastic kind. Personally, I put safflower or grapeseed oil in the bottle, but you can use which ever oil you like.

baking sheets, baking tins, rolling pin, parchment paper, kitchen timer, and more

In your essential baking tools stash include large stainless steel baking sheets, a loaf pan, a Bundt pan, a muffin tin, a mini-muffin tin—go wild! Get what you think you'll need, and if those silicon types float your boat, then get them too. You can use less oil with those. Make sure you always have parchment (not waxed) paper on hand, and a sturdy rolling pin. Additionally, make sure to get a digital timer or two—don't trust those winding ones. A metal frosting spatula can come in handy as well. If you don't trust your oven, grab a thermometer to make sure your oven is not running too hot.

Lastly, ice cream scoopers are really handy for easy scooping, for filling muffin tins and for measuring out cookie dough.

nonessential/optional

immersion blender

An immersion blender (stick or wand blender) can come in handy when you are pureeing soup inside the pot or don't want to break out the blender. The KitchenAid set comes with a four-cup mixing beaker, wire whisk, and nut chopper attachments, all in a nifty canvas bag.

suribachi with surikogi (or mortar and pestle)

This is like a Japanese mortar and pestle that has a large bowl filled with grooves. It's used to blend things by hand and make gomasio (sesame salt) and other condiments, like the *dulse pumpkin seed condiment*, on page 168. A mortar and pestle is great for blending spices, making curry pastes, and pureeing small jobs by hand.

flame deflector

A flame deflector can be used under a pot to help distribute the heat evenly across the pan. It can be helpful in cooking grains so the bottom doesn't burn.

pickle press

If you're interested in making pressed salads, your own pickles, or fermented foods, then grab a pickle press. These are usually a plastic container fitted with a lid that has an easy pressing knob that puts weight on whatever you're pressing. You can find presses online or at Japanese grocery stores.

tips for getting started

The best thing you can do to become a seasoned chef in your own kitchen is to practice, practice, practice! Take cooking classes to learn how to use a knife properly and to become skilled in various cooking techniques.

And, remember, eating simply is a good way to eat, so every meal doesn't have to be a gourmet cook-a-thon. If cooking plant-based meals seems daunting, a good way to start is to set a realistic goal for yourself each week. Learn basic cooking first, like how to make grains, cook vegetables in a tasty way, and how to make plant-based protein dishes with beans, tofu, and tempeh. Try at least two recipes out of this book per week, then go from there.

Making delicious, nourishing food can take some time, but if you plan your weekly meals and prep a few things beforehand, you'll shave several minutes off each recipe.

Here are some great tips of the trade to get you started making blissful meals while saving money and time:

- On Sunday, plan your menu for the week around what is available at the farmers market and what you already have in your pantry. If you have certain grains or beans stocked, use those up before you buy more. Write your weekly menu out in a notebook while making your shopping list. I find it's better to go to the store with a list so you don't end up wandering around aimlessly.

- Choose two days a week for "batch cooking," where you cook a large pot of grains and beans that you can use throughout the week. After all, it doesn't make sense to cook one cup of grains; you might as well make three cups, and then use it for various meals. For instance, out of one pot of brown rice you can make porridge for breakfast and sushi for lunch. Then you can use it in a grain salad for dinner, mixed into a soup for a one-pot meal, and in rice pudding for dessert. Finding crafty ways to use leftovers will not only save time and money, it will also encourage you to be creative in the kitchen.

- Get your vegetables washed, cut, and ready to go every few days. It's best if you buy veggies whole and cut them yourself. The precut veggies at the store have been cut and stored in a plastic bag for days, leaving them lifeless and tasteless. Cut your own and store them in airtight glass containers. Buy "green" bags to keep produce fresh for up to a week (as long as it hasn't been precut). These special bags can be found online or in most natural food stores and they really do work!

- Always wash grains, nuts, seeds, and beans before using in a recipe. They all have enzyme inhibitors on the outside, which prevent them from germinating too early; rinsing them washes this off. Also, if you are buying these items from the bulk bins (which I hope you are, since it reduces packaging and waste—plus it saves you money), they'll be dirty and possibly contain small stones that need to be picked out. To wash, put the food in a medium bowl, cover with water, and swirl your hand around, moving in a circle or a figure eight pattern. Drain and do the same thing again until the water is clear. You can use a mesh strainer after the final wash to catch anything that remains.

- Some of these items will need to be not just rinsed but soaked as well. In the grain and bean section, I specify which foods need to be soaked and which can go without. For those grains and beans that need to be soaked, rinse them thoroughly first, then cover them with water in a bowl right before you go to bed. You really can't over soak grains and beans, unless you leave them soaking for days. Cook them as soon as you wake up while you get ready for your day.

- Avoid the easy "junk food" way out. Do this by planning ahead and making sure that healthful food is always available to you. Have your pantry and fridge stocked, so when you come home from work you can easily figure out what to do for dinner. Also, if you have a tendency to run for the vending machine at work, make healthy snack foods to take with you like the *chewy trail mix bars*, on page 234. If healthy food is not easily accessible, you are more likely to make poor decisions on what to eat and miss out on bliss.

basic cooking and cutting techniques

you never make the same thing exactly the same

This is a funny thing about cooking. Everything you could possibly think of affects the food you make. Your mood, the weather, your environment, not to mention the quality of ingredients and where they came from, or how long they've been sitting in your pantry all affect how a recipe is going to turn out. Sometimes these things only have a small effect, but I wanted to put it out there for you to think about anyway. Another thing: If two people make the same exact recipe, the dish will come out differently for the same reasons I listed. Everyone has a different energy and personality, and that goes into the food. So your *coconut bliss granola parfait*, on page 35, is going to look and probably even taste a little different than mine, and that's okay. I want you to own that parfait, because it's made from your hands and that's pretty rad.

Go ahead and be creative. Don't feel like you have to stick to the recipe exactly. If something calls for zucchini, and you can't stand zucchini or only have broccoli, then give the broccoli a whirl or just leave it out completely. Don't feel trapped by these recipes. Recipes are building blocks or springboards that help guide you in making delicious, vibrant meals. If the recipe is a spring recipe but it's wintertime, then change the vegetables to whatever is in season at the moment and you have a whole new dish.

dried vs. fresh spices and herbs

Both dried and fresh herbs have their place in plant-based cooking—often in the same recipe. With dried herbs, you always want to add them to the recipe toward the beginning, either sautéed in oil or water, or blended into a sauce or dressing. Since they have been dried you must reconstitute them, which will bring out their flavor. You need more fresh herbs than dried herbs to get a concentrated flavor. For example, if a recipe calls for dried coriander, I might use a teaspoon or tablespoon. But if I wanted fresh coriander (cilantro), I would use more like one-quarter of a cup. With fresh herbs, you want to add them to the recipe toward the end or use them as a garnish.

toasting nuts and seeds

Adding nuts and seeds to a dish or using them as a garnish is an easy way to up the flavor, presentation, and nutrients of a recipe. I always buy raw nuts and seeds, then toast them myself in a skillet (rather than in the oven, where they are more likely to burn). Over a medium flame, heat up your skillet and add the nuts or seeds.

Make sure the flame is not too high. The pan doesn't need oil because the nuts already have plenty. Stir frequently or shake the pan back and forth. Try not to walk away from the pan for too long because they will burn before you know it! Keep stirring until the nuts are golden brown and fragrant. Depending on the nut and how much you chopped it (this should be done before adding them to the pan), this process could take anywhere from two to ten minutes.

seasoning to taste

Many recipes say season with sea salt to taste. This is because everyone's taste buds are different and my preferred level of salt is going to be different than yours. You will need to season the recipe to your preference, but remember it's always best to cook the salt/seasoning into the food rather than applying salt at the dinner table. Adding salt in the cooking

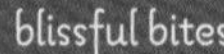

process brings out the natural flavor of the food, and you will end up using less salt in the long run (and we could all use a little less salt in our lives). Start with a little, and add a touch more as you go along. If you add too much at the beginning, it will be very difficult to fix the saltiness of the recipe.

Another way I season recipes is to use shoyu, tamari, or coconut aminos. Shoyu is a high-quality, unpasteurized soy sauce made by fermenting soybeans with water, salt, and wheat. Many of the brands found at Asian markets or regular grocery stores are high in sodium and contain alcohol. Try to find a high-quality shoyu or soy sauce that does not have alcohol. Tamari is the wheat-free version and is thicker and stronger in flavor than shoyu, so you can use less. I prefer tamari because it's gluten-free. Coconut aminos is the new kid on the block; it is raw, gluten-free, and soy-free. Experiment with all of these seasonings to see which you like best.

knife techniques

In an ideal world we would all be born with knife skills. Learning proper knife techniques can save you time, heartache, and frustration (and fingers in many cases). If possible, take a class near you or watch videos online. But the best way to learn knife skills is to practice. So get out that fancy new chef knife and get to choppin'! Below I describe the most commonly used cutting techniques.

chiffonade

A chiffonade is a fine slice or shred of leafy vegetables or herbs. You would use this cut for lettuce in salads, wraps, or tacos and with fresh herbs like basil. To chiffonade, simply stack a few leaves, roll them into a cigar shape, and slice. Remember to remove any tough, woody stems that you want to exclude from your preparation.

chop

Chopping a vegetable means it can be cut into chunks that do not need a uniform or specific shape. This is most commonly used for soups, stews, or anything that gets pureed.

diagonal

Also called a bias cut, cutting on the diagonal means you position your vegetable at a 45-degree angle on the cutting board while aiming your knife in the same direction as you cut. The angle to which you have your knife will determine how long the diagonal cut will be. I use this cut mostly for sautéed vegetables, stir-fry, and soups.

shredding

Shredding is usually done with cabbage and carrots for dishes like cole slaw, and can be done by hand or with a food processor. To shred

by hand, first remove the wilting outside leaves of the cabbage. Cut it in half down the center, then cut those pieces in half again. Carefully cut out the stalk. Put the flat side down on the cutting board and straight slice down one side of the cabbage until it's all in strips.

dicing

Dicing is cutting a vegetable into small cubed pieces. That usually means cutting the vegetable the long way first, then turning it to cut in the other direction. The size of your dice depends on how wide you cut these rows.

You would use this cut anytime you want your vegetable in uniform pieces.

half-moon/quarter-moon

This is achieved by cutting a round vegetable like a zucchini in half lengthwise, putting the flat side down, then cutting perpendicularly down the vegetable in whatever thickness you desire. To do a quarter-moon, cut the halved piece in half again lengthwise before cutting down the vegetable. This cut is beautiful and great for any dish.

julienne

This describes the cutting of vegetables into uniform, matchstick-sized pieces. Begin by neatly cutting the vegetable on the diagonal at about 45 degrees. Next, stack one to three pieces and slice into strips longways. If some

of your strips come out thicker than others, you can always go back and slice them thinner. You could use thicker matchsticks for sautés and thinner ones for raw salads.

mincing

Minced food is chopped finely into tiny bits. Mince the ingredients using a rocking or chopping motion, so that the front or tip of the blade maintains contact with the cutting board, while the back of the knife moves up and down, back and forth, doing the work. Use the sides of the knife to "pile" the ingredients repeatedly, as you continue mincing into very small particles. I use this technique for herbs and ginger.

prepping station

There is a saying in cooking known as *mise en place* (pronounced *meez an plahs*). This literally means "set in place" in French. It refers to having all your ingredients "in place" before you start your recipe.

So the first thing you do when trying out a new recipe is read the recipe once all the way through. This ensures that you know what steps will be happening so nothing sneaks up on you while you are cooking! It also helps you to have all the necessary equipment and tools for the recipe out on the counter. Then you get all your ingredients ready and put them all together near your cutting board, bowl, sauté pan, or whatever tools you are using to prepare the recipe. I call this the "prepping station." It's good to have out numerous glass bowls in a variety of sizes to hold your ingredients.

Start by measuring all the wet and dry ingredients, measuring out the spices, cutting the veggies, and whatever else you need to do for the recipe before combining ingredients. *Voilà*. It's all *mise en place!*

the recipes

"The only real stumbling block is fear of failure. In cooking you've got to have a what-the-hell attitude."

— Julia Child

mixed berry couscous surprise • 39

breakfast & brunch of champions

We often don't know what to eat for breakfast once we make the switch to a plant-based diet. We typically default to eating cereal and switch to soy, rice, or almond milk, but what if you want something more nutritious, or more captivating? And what about those times you want to impress your friends or make a lovely brunch for a loved one on their special day? These recipes give you healthy breakfast and brunch options, some of them being familiar, while others may be a new exploration for you.

spring

summer

autumn

winter

anytime

coconut bliss granola • 35

spring

coconut bliss granola

S • Makes 8 servings • **CHEF FAVE**

Store-bought granola is usually full of oil and sugar. Yet it's so easy to make yourself for half the cost—and half the guilt. You'll fall in love with this granola recipe, which you can serve with nondairy milk or with key-lime soy yogurt, *on this page. Store in an airtight container and it will last a few weeks.*

3 cups rolled oats
1 cup raw sunflower seeds
1 cup shredded dried coconut, unsweetened
1 cup brown rice crispy cereal
¾ cup sliced almonds
½ cup walnuts, chopped if whole
¼ cup sesame seeds
1 tablespoon cinnamon
Dash nutmeg
2 tablespoons grapeseed oil
½ cup maple syrup
1 teaspoon vanilla flavoring
Pinch sea salt
1 cup raisins (optional)

Preheat oven to 250 degrees F. Mix all dry ingredients, except raisins, in a large bowl. In a smaller bowl, whisk together wet ingredients. Pour wet ingredients into dry ingredients and combine thoroughly. Transfer to a 9x13 glass casserole dish and evenly smooth across the top. Bake for 45 minutes. Remove from oven and stir in raisins. Bake for another 10 minutes. Remove from oven and cool.

blissful suggestions

I prefer to use vanilla flavoring instead of vanilla extract because it can be found without alcohol and has a richer flavor. But if you can't find it or alcohol-free vanilla extract, you can substitute regular extract.

Always use raw unsalted nuts for recipes.

---

key-lime soy yogurt

G 45 • Makes 4 to 6 servings

This is tastier than store-bought vegan yogurt, but it's missing the acidophilus. No worries—you won't miss it, because it's still healthy and actually has no refined sugar like store brands.

2 packages Mori-Nu silken tofu
½ cup maple syrup or brown rice syrup
2 limes, zested and juiced
1 small lemon, juiced
1 teaspoon vanilla flavoring

Blend all ingredients in a food processor. Be sure to scrape the edges of the bowl a few times to incorporate all the tofu. Blend until smooth. Layer with *coconut bliss granola*, on page 35, and fresh berries for a parfait.

---

kamut crêpes

S • Makes about 6 crepes

Since going vegan, I find it impossible to get crêpes at a restaurant. So I decided to make a healthier version that has no refined sugar and uses kamut flour. This whole-grain flour can be found at natural food stores, but if you can't find it, try substituting spelt flour. Crêpe-making is an art and takes patience. The first or second time you do it will probably be a bust, so keep trying and you'll get the technique down in no time!

Oil spray, for pan
⅓ cup plus ½ cup water, as needed
½ cup rice milk
2 tablespoons maple syrup
1 tablespoon oil
½ cup kamut flour
¼ cup unbleached white flour
Pinch sea salt

Whisk together ⅓ cup water and the next six ingredients until well combined, with no lumps remaining. Let it sit in the fridge for 30 minutes. Whisk in more water as needed to get a very watery batter. Heat nonstick skillet over medium flame and spray lightly with oil. Pour in a small amount of batter (about ⅓ cup) while twisting the pan to spread a thin layer of batter across the bottom. Do this quickly, otherwise the crêpe will be too thick and not cook throughout. When it looks almost cooked through, carefully flip and cook on the other side until golden brown. Repeat with the remaining batter.

blissful suggestion

I prefer to use unsweetened, plain rice or almond milk in my recipes, but you are welcome to substitute any non-dairy milk. Soy milk is pretty neutral but keep in mind that hemp, oat, or hazelnut milks may change the taste of the recipe drastically.

---

lemon crème sauce

G 45 • Makes about 2 cups

This creamy sweet sauce is so tasty you might have to stop yourself from licking it right out of the bowl. But it's okay if you do because it's guilt-free! This egg-free, sugar-free sauce is lovely with crêpes, as a topping for pancakes or brownies, or served as layers of a parfait.

1 package Mori-Nu silken tofu
1 lemon, zested and juiced
½ tablespoon vanilla flavoring
⅓ cup maple syrup, or more to taste
1 tablespoon raw almond butter

fan ★ fave

pineapple cornbread muffins • 37

1 tablespoon unsweetened applesauce
1 tablespoon arrowroot

Blend all ingredients in a blender until well combined. Refrigerate up to five days.

---

pineapple cornbread muffins

 • Makes 1 dozen • **FAN FAVE**

I seriously could eat cornbread every day. I love it that much. This is a wheat-free breakfast cornbread muffin that is to die for when topped with Earth Balance and served with a cup of Earl Grey tea.

Oil spray, for pan
1½ cups cornmeal
1 cup barley flour (or other whole-grain flour)
¼ teaspoon sea salt
Dash cinnamon
1 teaspoon baking soda
1 teaspoon baking powder
⅓ cup unsweetened applesauce
⅔ cup unsweetened rice, almond, or soy milk
1 teaspoon apple cider vinegar
½ cup maple syrup
1 can (14 ounces) crushed pineapple in its own juice (or pineapple chunks)

Preheat oven to 350 degrees F. Spray muffin tin with oil or line with cupcake liners. Mix together dry ingredients in a large bowl. In separate bowl, whisk together the wet ingredients, then fold in pineapple. Add wet ingredients to dry ingredients and mix until well combined. Spoon into muffin tin until almost full. Bake for 30 to 35 minutes, or until a toothpick inserted in the center comes out clean. Let sit for five minutes then transfer to cooling rack.

nectarine cobbler smoothie • 39

summer

mixed berry couscous surprise

 • Makes 5 to 6 servings

This is probably the most kid-friendly dish in the cookbook, and adults will love it, too! It's a great alternative to breakfast cereal, or you could even serve it as a dessert if you add a bit of maple syrup.

2 cups whole-wheat couscous
1½ cups apple juice
1 cup filtered water
1 tablespoon fresh mint, chopped finely
1 cup strawberries, washed and sliced
½ cup raspberries, washed
½ cup blueberries, washed
1-2 teaspoons cinnamon
Fresh mint leaves, to garnish

Place couscous in a bowl. Mix together apple juice and water in a saucepan and bring to a boil. Pour liquid over couscous. Cover bowl with a towel or sushi mat and leave for about five minutes, or until all the liquid is absorbed. Fluff couscous with a fork, then gently stir in mint, berries, and cinnamon. Toss gently. Place in bowls and garnish with mint leaves.

nectarine cobbler smoothie

G 45 • Makes 1 smoothie

You'll be surprised how much this smoothie tastes like a cobbler in a cup—so delicious!

1 large nectarine, pit removed and chopped
1 container (6 ounces) plain soy yogurt, unsweetened
2 tablespoons maple syrup
4 ice cubes
Dash cinnamon, plus more for garnish

Combine all ingredients in a blender and blend until smooth and no lumps remain, about two to three minutes. Serve immediately. Garnish with a dash of cinnamon.

blissful suggestion

Alternatively, instead of a nectarine, you may use a large peach.

strawberry shortcake smoothie • 41

strawberry shortcake smoothie

 • Makes 2 smoothies

Strawberry shortcake has always been one of my favorite desserts. This smoothie gives me the taste of shortcake without all the carbs and calories. The best smoothies are made with frozen bananas, but if you don't have any frozen, add ⅓ cup ice.

2 cups unsweetened rice or almond milk
1 frozen banana (or 1 banana and ⅓ cup ice)
½ cup frozen or fresh strawberries
2 dashes cinnamon
1 tablespoon rice protein powder (optional)

Blend all ingredients until smooth and no lumps remain, about two minutes. Serve immediately.

sweet polenta porridge

G S 45 • Makes 3 to 4 servings

This is a new take on breakfast cereal. It's perfect for summer when you want a breakfast that is quick cooking yet nutritious and delicious. The kids will love it!

3 cups filtered water
1 cup yellow polenta, washed
2 pinches sea salt
⅓ cup unsweetened rice or almond milk
2 tablespoons raisins (optional)
Dash cinnamon
1 tablespoon sweetener, more or less to taste
½ cup walnuts, chopped and toasted (page 24)

Bring water and polenta to a boil in medium saucepan with sea salt. Simmer, whisking frequently for about 10 minutes, while polenta gets thick and creamy. Stir in milk, raisins, cinnamon, and sweetener to polenta. Whisk over low flame for a few minutes to incorporate the ingredients.

Pour into bowls immediately and sprinkle walnuts over porridge. Serve hot.

orange-pumpkin ginger french toast with roasted sweet and yukon potatoes • 43, 44

autumn

orange-pumpkin ginger french toast

S ◊ 45 • Makes 3 to 4 servings

After going vegan, it was hard to find a French toast recipe that I enjoyed, so I came up with my own. A fellow vegan blogger tipped me onto using ciabatta bread and it works best. If you don't have orange extract on hand, use the zest of one orange and one tablespoon of the juice, or just leave it out.

Oil spray, for pan
1 can (15 ounces) pumpkin, or 1 cup fresh pumpkin puree*
1 cup unsweetened almond or rice milk
1 teaspoon orange extract
1 teaspoon vanilla flavoring
1 tablespoon maple syrup
1 tablespoon arrowroot, dissolved in ½ cup rice milk
1 tablespoon flax meal
1-2 teaspoons ground ginger
½ teaspoon cinnamon
Pinch sea salt
1 loaf ciabatta bread, cut in ½ inch slices

In a medium bowl, whisk together all ingredients except oil and bread until well combined. Let sit for 10 minutes. Preheat oven to 350 degrees F and spray a baking sheet with oil. Dip each piece of bread in the batter, brush off the excess, and then place on cookie sheet. Continue with the rest of the bread. Bake for eight minutes, flipping each piece at the halfway point.

Heat skillet with oil over medium flame. Place as many pieces of bread that will fit in skillet and fry each side until medium brown or darker, about two minutes on each side. Continue with the rest of bread, spraying your pan with oil as needed.

blissful suggestion

Serve hot with vegan butter, organic maple syrup, and a sprinkle of cinnamon on top. These go great with *roasted sweet and yukon potatoes* on page 44.

blissful trick

Baking the bread first may seem unnecessary, but it helps dry it out so when you go to fry it, it doesn't stick to the pan or splatter everywhere.

to make pumpkin puree:

Take a two- to four-pound pumpkin, cut off the stem, then cut in half. Scoop out the seeds and stringy bits. Lay facedown in a casserole dish with 1 cup of water. Cover with foil. Bake pumpkin at 400 degrees F for 45 minutes, or until flesh is soft. Scoop out flesh from the skin and puree in a food processor until smooth. Refrigerate in airtight container up to one week or freeze in a plastic bag up to three months.

pumpkin spice pancakes

S 45 • Makes about 12 pancakes

This is a great way to use up that leftover pumpkin after Thanksgiving, or whenever you're in the mood for fancy pancakes. They are fluffy and not too sweet, so feel free to add more maple syrup to the wet ingredients.

Oil spray, for pan
1 cup whole grain flour (or mix whole grain with unbleached white flour)
2 teaspoons baking powder
1 teaspoon baking soda
Pinch sea salt
1 teaspoon pumpkin pie spice
1 tablespoon maple syrup
1½ cups unsweetened almond or rice milk
⅓ cup canned pumpkin or pumpkin puree (page 43)
1 tablespoon olive or coconut oil

Mix together dry ingredients. Whisk together wet ingredients in a separate bowl. Stir wet ingredients into dry ingredients. Combine thoroughly so no lumps remain. Heat skillet over medium flame. Spray pan with oil. Wait until the pan is hot before adding the pancake mix. When ready, pour about ¼ cup mix into skillet and allow it to sit until the sides begin to get firm and bubbly. Do not try to flip them too soon! Flip each cake, press down with a spatula, and cook for a few more minutes. Move them to a plate and repeat with the rest of the pancake batter. Serve with vegan butter and real maple syrup.

blissful trick

Pancakes work best cooked on a griddle or nonstick pan, but try to use a nontoxic, non-Teflon type if possible.

roasted sweet and yukon potatoes

G S 45 • Makes 3 to 4 servings

These are great for breakfast potatoes or as a side dish for any meal. I love sweet potatoes so much it made sense to use them in addition to yellow potatoes. Be sure to cut the potatoes about the same size so they cook evenly.

1 medium sweet potato, small cubes
2 cups Yukon Gold potatoes, small cubes
1 green bell pepper, cubed
Dash oil
Pinch sea salt
Dash nutritional yeast
½ teaspoon each of 2 to 3 spices of your choice: cumin, oregano, basil, paprika, coriander, rosemary, chili powder, black pepper

Preheat oven to 400 degrees F. Toss together all ingredients in a medium bowl, until the veggies are well covered with oil. Spread evenly on a baking sheet and bake until tender, tossing occasionally, about 45 minutes.

how to cut a bell pepper:

First slice off the bottom tip of the pepper. Face that side up and gently move your knife down each side along the seed pit. Then you can discard the pit and the little seeds aren't everywhere.

---

sizzling tempeh bacon

G • Makes 4 to 5 servings

You could buy store-bought Fakin' Bacon or you can make a healthier version at home. This "bacon," made with tempeh, is the perfect brunch side dish and is delicious sprinkled on top of salads.

1 package (8 ounces) tempeh
⅓ cup tamari
1 tablespoon liquid smoke
1 tablespoon toasted sesame oil
2 tablespoons maple syrup
1 tablespoon apple cider vinegar
1 teaspoon dried thyme
1 teaspoon paprika
Dash black pepper

Slice tempeh in half lengthwise, then in thin slices lengthwise. Whisk together the remaining ingredients in a glass dish large enough to fit slices of tempeh in one single layer. Coat tempeh and marinate for one hour, turning once.

Drain most of the marinade from the tempeh and save, leaving a little at the bottom of the pan. Bake for 30 to 35 minutes at 375 degrees F, turning once halfway through. If it looks dry at the halfway point, add a touch of the marinade to the pan.

blissful variation

You can also fry this bacon in a skillet over a medium flame to make it more reminiscent of real bacon.

blissful definition

Liquid smoke is a concentrated seasoning that gives a smoked flavor to the tempeh. It can be found at most grocery stores near the barbecue sauce. Just check to make sure it's vegan.

blissful tip: organic is the only way to go

The pesticides and chemicals used on food products today are not meant to be in our body. Not only do these unnatural chemicals strip nutrients from our food, harm the environment, and lead to soil depletion, but they also have been linked to cancer and Parkinson's, along with many other degenerative diseases, as well as autism. To avoid digesting these harmful substances, try to buy organic. If you are buying at a farmers market, you will see banners with a certified organic seal of approval. You can also talk with the farmers to see who is not spraying their produce but aren't yet certified. Certification is a lengthy and expensive process that many farmers aren't willing to bother with, but that doesn't mean you can't find delicious, pesticide-free produce from a nonorganic certified farmer. If you don't have a local farmers market, find the nearest natural food store, co-op, or Whole Foods Market in your area. If there are no natural food stores near you, ask your local grocery to carry organic produce. As the demand increases, the store will carry more organic items. Big retailers such as Target and Walmart and grocery stores such as Albertsons have added organic product lines in their stores. The way you can tell if a produce item is organic is to look at the label: *An organic produce label will have a five-digit number starting with 9, like 94013. Nonorganic produce has a four-digit number starting with a 4.*

The most heavily sprayed vegetable crops are celery; dark leafy greens such as kale, collards, and spinach; peppers; lettuce; potatoes; carrots; and zucchini; and fruits such as apples, berries, grapes, pears, cherries, nectarines, and peaches. These are called "The Dirty Dozen." If you can't buy *all* organic produce, be sure to avoid buying at least these items conventionally. Buy a veggie wash to clean them and any other conventionally grown produce to help reduce the amount of pesticides you consume.

gluten-free savory biscuits with apricot-blueberry fruit compote • 49

winter

gluten-free savory biscuits

G S ◊ 45 • Makes about 5 biscuits

People with a gluten intolerance shouldn't have to go without country-style biscuits! These are delicious and low in fat. Serve with apricot-blueberry fruit compote *(recipe follows) or* mushroom gravy *(page 150) for a savory treat.*

2 cups gluten-free all-purpose baking flour, plus more for rolling
½ cup brown rice flour
¾ teaspoon sea salt
1 tablespoon baking powder
¾ teaspoon baking soda
1 tablespoon coconut palm sugar
1 tablespoon flax seed meal
1 tablespoon arrowroot
2 tablespoons coconut oil
½ cup unsweetened rice milk, mixed with 1¼ teaspoon dry yeast
1 teaspoon apple cider vinegar
⅓ cup unsweetened applesauce

Preheat the oven to 450 degrees F. Place all the dry ingredients into a large bowl. Mix coconut oil into dry mix using a fork or your hands until the flour is crumbly and well combined. In a separate bowl, whisk together the rice milk and yeast and allow to sit for five minutes until it bubbles. Stir in vinegar and applesauce. Pour wet ingredients into dry ingredients and mix together until well combined.

Turn out onto a floured cutting board and make sure the dough stays together in a nice ball. Add more flour as needed if the dough is sticky.

With a rolling pin, roll the dough out to about 1½-inch thickness. Cut into rounds with a biscuit cutter and place on a baking sheet lined with parchment paper. Repeat with remaining dough. Bake for 12 minutes. Serve hot.

---

apricot-blueberry fruit compote

G S ◊ 45 • Makes about 1½ cups

Compote is a very Southern thing. My friends in L.A. would always make fun of me when I said it, because I would drag the word out: "compoooot." This makes a great topping for pancakes, scones, biscuits, toast, and grains—whether you say it with a Southern accent or not.

1 cup dried apricots, chopped
½ cup dried blueberries
1 cup filtered water
1 orange, zested and juiced
Pinch sea salt

1 teaspoon grated ginger
2 teaspoons maple syrup (optional)

Combine all ingredients in a small saucepan. Bring to a boil, then simmer with lid on until the fruit gets thick and is no longer watery, about 25 minutes. Check and stir frequently so the fruit doesn't stick. Remove lid toward the end of cooking to cook off any excess water. Remove from heat and serve.

---

maple almond-pecan scones

S 45 • Makes 8 scones

These aren't your typical scones made with white flour, tons of sugar, and butter. They are more healthy and wholesome yet really delicious, and will not send your blood sugar on a rollercoaster ride.

½ cup raw pecans
½ cup raw almonds
½ cup rolled oats
2 cups barley flour (or other whole-grain flour), plus more for pan
¼ teaspoon sea salt
1 tablespoon baking powder
1 teaspoon cinnamon
⅓ cup unsweetened applesauce
⅓ cup maple syrup, plus 2 tablespoons for topping
2 tablespoons safflower oil or coconut oil, melted
1 tablespoon vanilla flavoring
¼ cup chopped pecans or almonds

Preheat oven to 375 degrees F. Line a cookie sheet with parchment paper. Place first three ingredients in a food processor and process until mixture becomes a meal and no chunks remain. Transfer to a large mixing bowl and combine with the rest of the dry ingredients.

In a small bowl, mix together all the wet ingredients except for the 2 tablespoons maple syrup, then add to the dry ingredients; lastly, fold in the nuts. Mix together until it forms a firm dough ball—I usually use my hands toward the end. Sprinkle a little flour onto the parchment paper and transfer the dough to the sheet. Gently press the dough into an eight-inch circle, then cut into eight pieces with a sharp knife. You do not need to separate the wedges.

Glaze the tops with 2 tablespoons maple syrup. Bake for 15 to 20 minutes. Cool slightly, then transfer to a cooling rack. These are great alone or served with *apricot-blueberry fruit compote*, on page 49.

anytime

breakfast porridge with raisins

 • Makes 2 to 4 servings

This is a great porridge to make when you have grains left over. You can do any combination of grains, or all brown rice is good too.

1 cup cooked brown rice
1 cup cooked quinoa
1 cup unsweetened almond or rice milk
Handful raisins (optional)
Pinch sea salt
2 tablespoons maple syrup
Generous dash cinnamon
Walnuts, toasted, for garnish

Put all the ingredients, except the walnuts, in a saucepan and bring to a boil. Cover and reduce heat to a simmer. Cook until thick and creamy, about 10 minutes, stirring occasionally. Add more milk as necessary to get the consistency you prefer. Serve immediately in bowls garnished with nuts.

gluten-free banana walnut pancakes

G S 45 • Makes about 12 four-inch-round pancakes

Growing up with my dad, we only had pancakes made with Bisquick. I've come a long way since those days, and this pancake is the tastiest I've made since going vegan. You may need to add more milk (perhaps up to ½ cup more) to get the right consistency, so the pancakes cook all the way through.

Oil spray, for pan
1½ cups brown rice flour
1½ teaspoons baking powder
Pinch sea salt
½ teaspoon cinnamon
1½ cups unsweetened almond, rice, or soy milk
1 teaspoon apple cider vinegar
1 teaspoon oil
1 teaspoon vanilla flavoring
2 ripe bananas, mashed
½ cup walnuts or pecans (optional)

Whisk dry ingredients together in a medium bowl. Whisk together wet ingredients in a separate bowl. Mash banana well with a fork and stir into wet. Stir wet ingredients into dry ingredients and mix until well incorporated. Stir in nuts if using.

Heat skillet and spray with oil. Pour about ¼ cup pancake batter into skillet over medium flame. When you start to see bubbles forming and the edges getting done, it's time to flip the pancake. Heat on other side for two minutes and remove from skillet. Repeat with the rest of the pancake batter.

---

vegan "eggs" benedict

G 45 • Makes 4 to 6 servings

One of my favorite cafés in Los Angeles has a vegan benedict that needed some work so I decided to make my own version. I'm delighted by the way it turned out! I've never eaten real "eggs benedict" before, so I'm not sure how close this is to the real thing, but it doesn't really matter because it's awesome!

8 slices gluten-free bread, toasted
2 tomatoes, sliced ¼-inch thick
1 bunch kale, chopped and blanched
***Southwest tofu scramble* (page 53) made with 1 teaspoon each of oregano and marjoram instead of cumin and chili powder**

no-oil hollandaise sauce

makes about 2 cups

1 package Mori Nu silken tofu
½ cup nutritional yeast
1 tablespoon white or yellow miso
2 tablespoons tamari
1 lemon, juiced
½ teaspoon turmeric
Dash black pepper
½ teaspoon paprika
1 tablespoon arrowroot
Unsweetened nondairy milk, as needed (to thin sauce)

Blend all sauce ingredients in a blender until smooth and no lumps remain.

to assemble the benedict:

Place toasted bread on a plate. Layer with tomato slices and kale, then tofu scramble.

Top with *no-oil hollandaise sauce*. Serve immediately.

blissful variation

Layer in *sizzling tempeh bacon*, on page 45, on top of bread.

blissful definition

Miso is a fermented soybean paste that has been traditionally used in Asia for making soup stocks. It offers many health benefits. Miso comes in a wide range of flavors—the darker misos have been fermented longer, have richer flavors, and are more nutritious. Be sure to never boil miso, because that kills the enzymes and healing properties that are naturally inside.

blissful trick

If you're not familiar with blanching, see page 107 for info on various cooking techniques.

vegan "eggs" benedict • 52

southwest tofu scramble

G 45 • Makes 4 to 6 servings

This will be the best tofu scramble you have ever tasted—I promise. The trick is to use a nonstick pan (the nontoxic kind) and let the tofu cook on one side until it gets brown before flipping.

Oil spray, for skillet
1 package (14 ounces) extra firm tofu, pressed if needed, then crumbled
⅓ cup nutritional yeast
2 tablespoons tamari
1 teaspoon cumin
1 teaspoon chili powder
1 medium carrot, small dice
Pinch sea salt
1 cup zucchini, small dice
5 mushrooms, sliced

In a large bowl, combine the first five ingredients until thoroughly mixed; set aside.

Meanwhile, spray skillet with oil and sauté carrots with a pinch of sea salt until almost tender. Add zucchini and mushrooms and sauté for two more minutes with lid on. Remove from pan and set aside.

Spray the same pan with oil spray and heat again over medium flame. Layer tofu mixture along the bottom of the pan about ½-inch thick (you may have to cook the tofu in two batches depending on the size of your pan). Let sit for five minutes before flipping. Cook on the other side until golden brown. Stir in veggies and serve immediately.

blissful variation

This is excellent served as a sandwich for the kids or wrapped in a tortilla for a quick lunch.

"Live each season as it passes; breathe the air, drink the drink, taste the fruit, and resign yourself to the influences of each."

— H.D. Thoreau

mango-pineapple tropical soup • 69

appetizers and soups for every occasion

Whether you are entertaining for a large party, need a quick snack, or crave a hot bowl of steaming soup, these recipes are great for any and every occasion. Even if you just want something fancy to eat while veggin' out in your pajamas.

spring

summer

autumn

winter

anytime

fan ★ fave

lemony-lime hummus • 60

spring

a taste of india artichoke dip

G [icon] 45 • Makes 4 to 6 servings

This appetizer is an efficient way to use leftover beans and great for a party for any occasion. It's full of Indian spices and ginger, but I wouldn't say it's hot. It's mild to medium, so if you want it spicier, feel free to add a touch of cayenne to it.

1 can (14 ounces) artichoke hearts, drained
1½ cups cooked chickpeas, or 1 can (15 ounces) drained and rinsed
1 tablespoon mirin
1 tablespoon brown rice vinegar or apple cider vinegar
2 teaspoons maple syrup
2 tablespoons tamari
2 teaspoons garam masala
1 teaspoon ginger, grated
Sea salt, pinch
Nutritional yeast, for topping (optional)
Baguette, sliced

Place all the dip ingredients in a food processor and blend until all the ingredients are well combined and no chunks remain. Be sure to scrape down the edges of the bowl a few times to incorporate all the ingredients. Transfer to a serving bowl and sprinkle nutritional yeast on top. Toast baguette and serve with dip.

blissful suggestion

To make beans from scratch follow *basic beans* recipe, on page 202.

blissful definitions

Mirin is Japanese cooking wine that is slightly sweet and has a low alcohol content. It's great to use as a substitute for cooking wine or sherry. I also use it in sauces, dressing, glazes, and dishes like this dip to add depth.

Brown rice vinegar is made from cultured brown rice, making it a healthier choice than regular rice vinegar. It has a nicer flavor as well. It can be found at any natural food store, but feel free to substitute another vinegar if you can't find it.

lemony-lime hummus

G S ◊ 45 • Makes 5 to 7 servings • **FAN FAVE**

This is my favorite way to have hummus—with both lemon and lime and no oil. This is a great way to use leftover beans. You can use it as a dip or a spread for a sandwich or wrap.

2 cups cooked garbanzo beans, or 2 cans (15 ounces each), drained and rinsed
1 clove garlic, minced (optional)
1 small lemon, zested and juiced
1 small lime, zested and juiced
1 teaspoon cumin
1 teaspoon coriander
1 teaspoon chili powder
1 tablespoon apple cider vinegar
1 to 2 tablespoons tahini (roasted for richer flavor)
Pinch black pepper
Filtered water, as necessary
Season to taste

Combine all ingredients in food processor. Blend, adding filtered water, or garbanzo cooking liquid, as necessary to get the texture and creaminess you desire. Season with sea salt.

blissful variation

If you want a kick, add ¼ teaspoon cayenne pepper.

curried split pea soup

G 45 • Makes 6 to 8 servings

This is a great soup to make in your pressure cooker. Split pea soup usually takes more than 30 minutes to make, but this one only takes 10 minutes!

2 teaspoons safflower oil
1 teaspoon whole cumin seeds
1 teaspoon fennel seeds
1 teaspoon ginger, minced
Pinch sea salt
2 cups green split peas, picked over and rinsed
6 cups filtered water
2 tablespoons mild curry powder
1 cup light coconut milk
1 cup spinach
Tamari, to taste
Cilantro, for garnish

Heat oil in pressure cooker over medium flame. Sizzle the cumin and fennel for a few minutes. Stir in ginger and sea salt. Add split peas, water, and curry powder. Stir well.

Lock lid on pressure cooker and set to highest setting. Over high heat, bring to pressure. Lower heat enough to maintain high pressure and cook for six minutes. Let the pressure come down naturally. Remove lid. Stir in coconut milk and spinach, cooking over low heat. Add tamari to taste. Serve in bowls garnished with cilantro.

hearty lentil soup

G • Makes 6 to 8 servings

Lentils are a fiber-rich member of the legume family that are easy to cook in a variety of ways. Lentils are great for blood-sugar disorders because their high fiber content helps prevent blood sugar levels from rising too quickly.

1 tablespoon sesame oil
½ onion, diced (optional)
Pinch sea salt
2 medium carrots, chopped
2 celery stalks, diced
1 tablespoon oregano
7 cups spring water
2 bay leaves
1 cup green lentils, washed and drained
1-inch piece fresh ginger, minced
2 tablespoons tamari
2 tablespoons miso, any variety
2 tablespoons lemon juice
Parsley, chopped, for garnish
Season to taste

Heat oil in stockpot over a medium flame. Sauté onion with sea salt until translucent. Add carrot, celery, and oregano and sauté for a few minutes with lid on. Stir in water, bay leaves, lentils, and ginger. Bring to a boil. Reduce flame and simmer with lid until lentils are tender, about 35 minutes. Stir occasionally. Add tamari and continue to simmer for three to five minutes. Remove bay leaves.

Turn off flame. In a small bowl or tea cup, dilute miso with a little cooking liquid . Stir miso and lemon juice into soup and let sit for five minutes. Taste to see if more sea salt is needed. Serve garnished with chopped parsley.

sweet carrot-ginger bisque

G S 45 • Makes 5 to 7 servings

Carrots are jam-packed with vitamin A and beta-carotene, making them excellent veggies for vision and protection against cancers. And since they are naturally sweet, carrots are great at regulating blood sugar. The oil is optional, so feel free to use water if you want to reduce the fat.

1 tablespoon coconut oil or ½ cup water
3 cups sliced carrots (about 4 medium carrots)
1 teaspoon cumin
1 teaspoon coriander
1 teaspoon paprika
4 cups filtered water, or more as needed
2 cups unsweetened almond or rice milk (soy milk can be used)
2 tablespoons brown rice syrup or maple syrup
2 tablespoons ginger juice*
2 tablespoons nutritional yeast
Pinch cayenne (optional)
Pinch black pepper
Sea salt, to taste
Fresh herbs, for garnish

Heat oil or ½ cup water in medium stockpot over medium heat. Add carrots and sauté for two minutes with lid on. Add spices and sauté for two more minutes. Stir in water and almond milk and bring to a boil. Simmer until carrots are soft, about 20 minutes. Let cool slightly, then puree with an immersion blender or in a conventional blender. Return to pot. Stir in all remaining ingredients except fresh herbs. Season to taste. Cook for five more minutes over low flame or until hot. Serve immediately garnished with fresh herbs.

to make ginger juice:

Grate a 1-inch piece of ginger with a Microplane zester or Japanese ceramic grater, then squeeze out the juice.

love your heart beet soup • 63

blissful suggestion

Since this soup is being pureed, your veggies don't need to be cut nicely, just chopped. But the smaller you cut them, the faster this soup will cook, and it's best if they are uniform in size.

---

love your heart beet soup

G ◊ 45 • Makes 5 to 7 servings

If you thought you didn't like the earthy, rich flavor of beets, you must try this soup. Similar to Russian borscht, this creamy soup uses red lentils for extra protein with no saturated fat. This soup also uses umeboshi vinegar, which may be new to you, but these Japanese pickled plums have been used medicinally in Asia for centuries.

1 tablespoon coconut oil or ½ cup water
2 medium carrots, chopped
2 medium red beets, peeled and chopped
1 tablespoon coriander
1 teaspoon oregano
Pinch sea salt, plus more to taste
5 cups filtered water
1 cup red lentils, washed and drained
1 tablespoon umeboshi vinegar or red wine vinegar
1 small lemon, juiced
Dash black pepper
Soy sour cream, for topping
Chopped dill, for garnish
Sea salt, to taste

Heat oil or ½ cup water in a large stockpot over medium flame. Add carrots, beets, and spices with a pinch of sea salt and sauté for four minutes covered, stirring occasionally. Add water and lentils. Bring to a boil, then lower flame. Simmer partially covered for about 25 minutes, or until lentils are cooked through.

Puree in small batches in a blender and return to pot. Or use an immersion blender. Stir in vinegar, lemon, and pepper. Taste and add sea salt if needed.

Serve warm or cold garnished with a dollop of soy sour cream and chopped dill.

blissful definition

Umeboshi plums are pickled plums from Japan that are used to make umeboshi vinegar. The plums have many medicinal properties. *Umeboshi vinegar* is the liquid left over from the pickling process, which can be used as a seasoning. It's very salty, so use sparingly.

cali-style white bean bruschetta • 65

summer

cali-style white bean bruschetta

 • Makes 5 to 7 servings

Some people stay away from avocados because they are high in fat. But the fat in avocados is monounsaturated, which studies show may lower cholesterol. So don't be scared! Try this new take on the Italian appetizer bruschetta, made with white beans for added fiber.

2 cups cooked white navy beans, or 2 cans (15 ounces each), drained and rinsed
1 large avocado, small cubes
⅓ cup packed fresh basil, chiffonade (page 27)
½ cup cherry tomatoes, quartered
Splash olive oil (optional)
2 tablespoons balsamic vinegar
Sea salt, to taste
Baguette slices

Mix bruschetta ingredients together and let marinate for at least 30 minutes in the fridge. Taste, and season with sea salt as necessary. Toast bread and pile it on.

blissful variation

This can be served in lettuce or cabbage leaves if you're avoiding bread, or just eat it on its own with a side of grains.

blissful suggestion

To make beans from scratch follow *basic beans* recipe, on page 202.

---

easy guacamole

 • Makes about 2½ cups

This is quick and easy guacamole that isn't spicy. If you want to make it spicy, feel free to add chopped jalapeños or a touch of cayenne pepper.

3 small ripe avocados, cubed
1 tablespoon fresh lime juice
¼ teaspoon cumin
¼ teaspoon chili powder
Pinch black pepper and sea salt
⅓ cup tomatoes, chopped (optional)

1 tablespoon cilantro, chopped
Season to taste

Mash avocados in a small bowl with a fork until you obtain the consistency you prefer. I like it a little chunky. Stir in the rest of ingredients and season to taste.

---

six- (or seven-) layer dip

45 • Makes about 10 servings

This recipe makes enough to fill a 9x13 dish, but if you want less, you can always halve the recipe. I would consider this party food, not something you would eat all the time. It will be the biggest hit at your next party or potluck. For a seven-layer dip, sprinkle black olives on top.

1 cup dried pinto beans, or 2 cans (15 ounces each), drained and rinsed
Filtered water
1 package Soyrizo
1 tub (12 ounces) soy sour cream
1 jar of your favorite salsa
***Easy guacamole*, on page 65**
1 small head romaine lettuce, chiffonade (see cutting techniques on page 27)
2 cups cherry tomatoes, sliced in half
1 package (8 ounces) Daiya cheese (optional)
1 cup olives, chopped (optional)

Follow *basic beans* recipe, on page 202, if using dried beans. After the beans are done, drain and mix with Soyrizo. While the beans are cooking, get the rest of the ingredients for the layers ready. Mix sour cream with salsa in a medium bowl until well combined. Make the guacamole.

Get all your dip layers together and start layering in your casserole dish.

The bottom layer is the bean/soyrizo mix. Spread evenly across the bottom of the pan. Second, spread the sour cream/salsa mix evenly across the beans. Third, gently smooth the guacamole over the salsa mix. Fourth, sprinkle the lettuce evenly over the guacamole. Fifth, sprinkle the tomatoes evenly over the lettuce. Lastly, sprinkle Daiya cheese, if using, all over the top. If you love olives, then sprinkle them over the top of the dip. Serve with your favorite non-GMO corn tortilla chips.

---

chilled corn bisque

G 45 • Makes 3 to 4 servings

This soup is so awesome, easy, and tasty! Perfect on a hot summer day served with a sandwich like the tempeh reuben, *on page 185.*

2½ cups unsweetened almond milk (or made fresh)
4 cups fresh corn, off the cob, shaved
1½ cups avocado
1 tablespoon tamari
1 tablespoon nutritional yeast
Pinch sea salt and black pepper
Parsley, for garnish
Chopped tomatoes, for garnish

Blend first five ingredients in a food processor or blender until smooth and creamy. Chill for at least 15 minutes before serving. Garnish with chopped parsley and tomatoes.

chilled corn bisque • 66

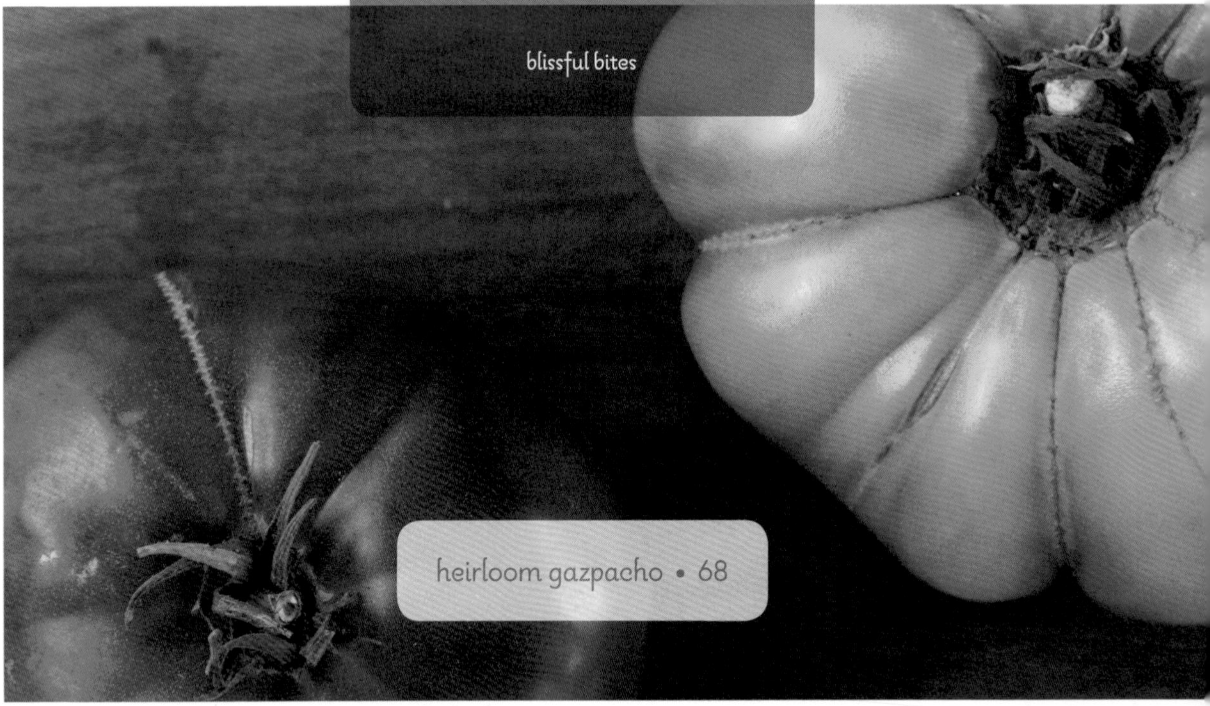

heirloom gazpacho • 68

blissful suggestion

You can vary up this soup by adding different spices depending on your mood. For a Mexican twist, add 1 teaspoon each cumin and chili powder and garnish with cilantro instead of parsley. Or for an Indian twist, add ½ teaspoon each curry powder and coriander.

---

heirloom gazpacho

 • Makes 4 to 6 servings

One of my favorite fruits available at the farmers market in the summer is the heirloom tomato. They sure are expensive, but their taste is unparalleled, deep and rich. If you can't find heirloom tomatoes, you can substitute Roma for this summer favorite.

4 large heirloom tomatoes, chopped (about 4 cups)
½ English or hothouse cucumber, peeled and chopped (about 1 cup)
1 red bell pepper, cored, seeded, and chopped
1 green bell pepper, cored, seeded, and chopped
½ cup fresh cilantro, chopped
1 lime, juiced
½ tablespoon Tabasco or 1 teaspoon chopped jalapeño
¼ cup balsamic vinegar
Sea salt, to taste

Blend first eight ingredients in a blender until it's the consistency you prefer. Season with sea salt to taste. Chill for at least 15 minutes before serving.

curry-red lentil corn chowder

G 45 • Makes 5 to 7 servings

This is one of the most satisfying soups in this cookbook, in my opinion. Miso has many medicinal properties and is one of my favorite ways to season soups. Feel free to add more spices if you want to kick it up a notch.

1 tablespoon coconut oil or ⅓ cup water
2 tablespoons shallots, finely chopped (optional)
1 celery stalk, small dice
1 red bell pepper, chopped
Pinch sea salt
1 tablespoon cumin
1 teaspoon oregano
1 tablespoon curry powder
1 cup dried red lentils, sorted for stones and washed
6 cups filtered water
2 cups fresh corn kernels (or frozen is fine)
3 tablespoons white miso, dissolved
Small handful parsley, chopped
1 tablespoon red wine vinegar
Sea salt, to taste

Heat oil or water in medium stockpot over medium heat. Add shallots, celery, red bell pepper, and sea salt and cook for a few minutes. Stir in spices and cook for three minutes more. Add lentils and water to the pot and bring to a boil. Add corn and simmer for 20 minutes, until lentils get soft and creamy. If using frozen corn, add it after lentils have cooked through. Turn off heat.

Dissolve miso in a small amount of water and stir into soup. Add parsley and vinegar, and season with sea salt if necessary.

blissful variation

Add ½ cup quinoa and 1 more cup of water with the lentils for a delicious one-pot meal.

---

mango-pineapple tropical soup

G S 45 • Makes 4 to 6 servings

Chilled raw soups are some of my favorite things about summer. So quick and easy to make, they have all kinds of nutrients and good things. If you want this spicier, throw in chopped jalapeño to your liking.

1½ cups cucumbers, chopped
1 cup pineapple, fresh or frozen
1 cup mango, peeled and chopped (frozen mango is fine)
1 lime, zested and juiced
1 tablespoon maple syrup
½ teaspoon sea salt
Handful cilantro
1 cup water
Pinch cayenne (optional)

Blend all ingredients until smooth. Serve chilled.

blissful tip: a word about genetically modified foods

Be sure that the organic foods you buy have not been genetically modified. The most common genetically modified (GMO) foods are corn, soybeans, canola, some flax, and squashes. According to *bio.org*, "at least 70 percent of processed foods on grocery store shelves contain ingredients and oils from biotech crops." In the U.S., these foods are not labeled, so you have to watch out. Though there is no long-term evidence on how GMO foods react in our body, we *do* know that farmers located near GMO crops are losing profits due to cross-contamination of their crops. And many of these farmers and their families are getting diseases, such as cancer, from the contaminated groundwater. Many documentaries (such as *Future of Food* and *The World According to Monsanto*) shed light on the GMO situation and the damages caused by Monsanto, the leader in GMO foods. Many countries won't buy certain produce from America because they worry about biotech ingredients in our food. Vote with your dollar and do not buy GMO products.

daikon canapé with sweet miso sauce • 72

pineapple-cucumber gazpacho

  • Makes 3 to 5 servings

I used to have a soup like this in the summer at a local café. That version had too much raw onion, so I made my own with the perfect amount. Very simple to make, this is a soup you'll love all summer long.

2 English cucumbers, peeled and chopped
1½ cups green bell pepper, seeded and chopped
1 green onion, chopped (optional)
2 tablespoons tamari
1 cup cilantro
1 can (29 ounces) pineapple with juice (or 1½ cups fresh pineapple with 1 cup water)
1 teaspoon cumin
2 tablespoons lemon juice
2 tablespoons lime juice
Sea salt and black pepper, to taste
Pineapple rings, for garnish (optional)

Blend all ingredients in a blender for about five minutes, or until no chunks remain. Chill for at least 15 minutes before serving. Decorate with pineapple rings.

blissful variation

For a kick, add 1 tablespoon chopped jalapeño and fresh mint.

autumn

daikon canapé with sweet miso sauce

G 45 • Makes about 20 pieces

This is one of my favorite appetizer recipes from the French Meadows Cookbook, *by Julie Ferré. Every year I go to the French Meadows Summer Camp in Northern California, where the food is amazing and the people are even sweeter. I hope you'll come visit us at camp sometime! Learn more about it in the resources section.*

1 daikon radish, approximately 10 inches long, 1-inch rounds
2 cups filtered water for blanching
Pinch sea salt
Parsley, for garnish

sweet miso sauce

makes about ¼ cup

1 tablespoon unrefined sesame oil
3 tablespoons brown or white rice miso
½ teaspoon brown rice vinegar
½ teaspoon brown rice syrup

Slice daikon into thin rounds. Bring water to a boil in a small saucepan. Add sea salt and return to a boil. Add rounds of daikon radish, up to 10 at a time into the water. Bring to a boil and cook to desired tenderness. Daikon holds its shape well, and can be blanched for 15 seconds, cooked al dente for one minute, or simmered longer, up to three minutes. Remove, drain, and separate pieces to cool. Repeat with remaining rounds of daikon.

In the meantime, prepare *sweet miso sauce.* In a small saucepan, heat sesame oil briefly. Add miso and sauté until aromatic, 30 seconds to one minute. Remove from heat and stir in other ingredients. Mix well.

to serve the canapé:
Serve ½ teaspoon *sweet miso sauce* on top of daikon round. Tuck cilantro or parsley leaf into sauce for flash of color. Additional adornments include roasted sesame seed or blanched carrot, cut julienne.

---

citrus coconut-kabocha bisque

G S 45 • Makes 5 to 7 servings

This orange-kissed soup is one of my go-to fall dishes. Kabocha is my favorite hard-skinned squash, but if you can't find it, substitute butternut. Kabocha is a Japanese pumpkin that helps regulate blood sugar because of its high fiber content.

1 tablespoon coconut oil
1 medium kabocha squash, seeded and cubed

citrus coconut-kabocha bisque • 72

Pinch sea salt
1 orange, zested and juiced
5 or more cups filtered water
1 can (13½ ounces) coconut milk
Pinch white pepper
Fresh herbs, for garnish
Sea salt, to taste

Heat oil in medium stockpot. Sauté the kabocha with sea salt for about three minutes, covered, stirring occasionally. Add a little water if the kabocha starts to stick to the pan. Add orange zest and juice. Sauté for two more minutes.

Add water and coconut milk and bring to boil. Simmer until kabocha is very soft (about 20 minutes). Puree with immersion blender right in the pot or in batches in a regular blender (return to pot when finished blending). Add pepper and sea salt to taste. Serve hot garnished with herbs.

---

raw pear-walnut bisque

 • Makes 5 to 7 servings

I randomly came up with this soup at a friend's potluck. I had never used walnuts for the base of a raw soup before and they created a rich, thick texture that was perfect for fall. The lemon zest adds a nice zing. It can be served warm right out of the blender or chilled.

2 cups walnuts, soaked 3 hours
1½ cups filtered water
2 cups Bosc pears, cored and sliced (about 2 pears)
1 tablespoon tamari
2 teaspoons apple cider vinegar
2 tablespoons lemon zest
2 tablespoons lemon juice
Sea salt, to taste

Drain walnuts. Start by blending water with walnuts for a few minutes. Add the rest of the ingredients and blend until completely smooth and no chunks remain. This could take anywhere from three to eight minutes depending on your blender. Taste and add sea salt, if needed.

---

thyme for miso

G 45 • Makes 4 to 6 servings

This soup is really good during fall because you can get fresh butternut squash. In other seasons you can substitute other veggies for the squash.

5 cups filtered water
2 cups butternut squash, peeled and cubed small
1 cup carrot, large dice
2 teaspoons dried thyme
Pinch sea salt
1 to 2 tablespoons wakame, cut into little pieces
1 tablespoon barley miso
1 tablespoon yellow or white miso

Combine water, veggies, and thyme in a medium saucepan and bring to a boil with a pinch of salt. Reduce to a simmer, cover, and cook until the veggies are tender, about five to seven minutes. Add wakame and simmer another minute. Turn off flame. Mix miso with about ¼ cup of the soup broth until well dissolved. Stir into pot and let sit for a few minutes. Stir well and serve.

blissful suggestion

If you reheat this soup the next day be sure not to boil the miso. Boiling kills the beneficial qualities of the miso.

curried sweet potato and carrot soup • 75

curried sweet potato and carrot soup

G 45 • Makes 3 to 5 servings

This soup is the perfect fall treat when the farmers markets are full of root vegetables. A great timesaver for the future is to make a double batch and freeze in the freezer.

1 tablespoon coconut oil or ½ cup water
3 cups sweet potatoes, cut into chunks
2 cups carrots, cut into chunks
Pinch sea salt
1 tablespoon curry powder, or more to taste
½ teaspoon cinnamon
1 teaspoon coriander
5 or more cups filtered water
1 tablespoon sweet white miso, dissolved in ¼ cup water
Sea salt, to taste
Handful parsley or cilantro, for garnish

Heat oil or water in large saucepan or stockpot. Add sweet potatoes and carrots with a pinch of sea salt and sauté for three minutes. Add the spices and sauté until well coated. Add water and bring to a boil. Cover and simmer 15 minutes, until vegetables are soft.

Let soup cool slightly. Puree the soup in a blender (or with immersion blender) until smooth and creamy, and then return it to pot. Dissolve miso in hot water and stir into soup. Simmer three to four minutes. Season to taste. Serve hot, garnished with chopped parsley or cilantro.

save a duck pâté • 77

winter

citrus herb cashew crudités

   45 • Makes 4 to 6 servings

I made this beautiful appetizer platter and herb dip for a friend's reunion party in January. It was the perfect thing to serve to her "omni" friends; rich, creamy, tasty—but healthy with no oil or added fat. Feel free to add water to get the consistency you prefer. I kind of like it a bit chunky, but you may find you like it smoother.

1 cup raw cashews
½ cup raw pumpkin seeds
Palm-size handful of fresh basil and parsley
2 tablespoon nutritional yeast
1 tablespoon lemon zest
2 tablespoons lemon juice
1 tablespoon white miso
2 tablespoons filtered water, or more as needed
Pinch sea salt
Veggies of your choice

Soak cashews and pumpkin seeds for two hours. Drain and combine with all ingredients, except veggies, in a food processor. Blend until well combined or to your desired consistency. Be sure to scrape down the edges of the bowl a few times to incorporate all the ingredients. Serve on a platter with sliced veggies of your choice.

blissful definition

Crudités is a French word that is an appetizer of raw veggies with some sort of dip. It's the perfect party dish and looks beautiful too. I like to serve this spread with carrot sticks, cucumber slices, cherry tomatoes, celery sticks, and broccoli florets.

---

save a duck pâté

  45 • Makes 3 to 4 servings

This protein-rich pâté is made from tempeh, which is a fermented soybean product full of fiber that won't clog your arteries. Serve this with crackers or pita bread at your next party, and I guarantee it will be a hit!

1 package (8 ounces) tempeh, cubed
½ cup almonds, roasted
1 tablespoon Dijon mustard
1 tablespoon lemon juice
1 tablespoon balsamic vinegar

azuki bean and japanese pumpkin soup • 78

3 tablespoons filtered water
1 tablespoon white miso
2 tablespoons nutritional yeast
1 teaspoon tamari
Pinch sea salt
4 tablespoons fresh dill
Handful cilantro or parsley
Crackers and/or veggies of your choice

Steam tempeh for 10 minutes. Process almonds until fine in a food processor, then add tempeh and blend for two minutes. Add the rest of the pâté ingredients and process until smooth. Be sure to scrape around the edges of the bowl a few times to incorporate all the ingredients. Form into a shape or loaf and serve on a platter with crackers or rice cakes, and veggies.

azuki bean and japanese pumpkin soup

G • Makes 4 to 6 servings

The Japanese use azuki beans for their many health benefits, including improved blood circulation and reduced fatigue, detoxified body (skin and organs), and a healthy digestive system.

1½ cups azuki beans, washed and soaked 6 to 8 hours
5 cups water
2 bay leaves
2 cups kabocha squash, small cube
Pinch sea salt

4 cups vegetable broth
2 large carrots, chopped
2 tablespoons white miso, diluted in ¼ cup soup broth
½ cup minced parsley or cilantro (save some for garnish)
White pepper, pinch
Sea salt, to taste

Combine azuki beans with water and bay leaves in a stockpot and bring to a boil. Simmer with lid on for 40 minutes, or until azuki gets tender but not mushy. Add squash, salt, and broth, and simmer for 20 minutes. Add carrots and simmer for five more minutes.

Dilute miso in a small amount of broth and add to pot. Simmer for one minute more, then turn off flame. Stir in fresh herbs, white pepper to taste, and sea salt to taste if needed. Serve garnished with fresh herbs.

---

winter white bean stew

G S ⌂ 45 • Makes 4 to 6 servings

In the winter time all I want is a warming, comforting soup. White beans have such a rich flavor with very little fat. This stew hits the spot and is full of fiber, vitamins, and minerals.

1 cup dried cannellini beans, soaked 6 to 8 hours
1-inch piece of kombu
3 cups filtered water
1 cup onion, diced
1 tablespoon coriander
1 tablespoon tarragon
2 bay leaves
2 cups garnet yam, 1-inch cubes
1 can (14½ ounces) diced tomatoes
1 tablespoon lemon juice
2 tablespoons cashew butter
1 cup filtered water
2 cups collard greens, cut in strips
Season to taste

Drain beans. Place the first nine ingredients in a pressure cooker, lock lid, put on high setting, then bring up to pressure over a high flame. When up to pressure, lower flame and simmer for 25 minutes. Turn off flame and let cooker come down from pressure. Remove lid. Whisk together the cashew butter with a little of the soup broth until well dissolved. Stir in the rest of ingredients with cashew butter and simmer for five more minutes. Season to taste and serve hot.

blissful suggestion

If you don't have a pressure cooker (or don't want to cook the beans from scratch in a pot) you can substitute 2 (14-ounce) cans of white beans, rinsed and drained. Add them with the cashew butter.

asian rice paper rolls • 81

anytime

asian rice paper rolls with almond bliss dipping sauce

G · O · 45 • **CHEF FAVE**

The amount of fillings you need to cut depends on how many rolls you want. These rolls don't keep long once made, so make only what you need. Don't overstuff them; you want them no more than two inches in diameter.

Rice paper for soft rolls
Warm water

your favorite fillings

Thin rice noodles, cooked according to package instructions
Napa cabbage and red cabbage, thinly sliced
Carrots, matchsticks
Basil, cilantro, mint
Bean sprouts
Pan-fried tofu or tempeh
Fruit (such as a mango, peach, or pear), sliced
Ripe avocado, sliced

almond bliss dipping sauce

makes about ½ cup

⅓ cup unsalted creamy almond butter
3 tablespoons tamari
3 tablespoons brown rice vinegar
2 tablespoons maple or brown rice syrup
1 teaspoon grated ginger
¼ cup filtered water, as necessary, to obtain desired consistency

Prepare your spring roll station by getting all your equipment ready, including a bowl of water for dipping the rice paper in, a plate or cutting board to roll on, and a platter to put your finished rolls on.

Start by dipping the entire piece of rice paper in the water, then pulling it out right away (do not leave it sitting in water; it will soften up more as you work). Lay the rice paper on the plate and layer in ingredients toward the bottom side closest to you in the middle, leaving a couple of inches clear on either side of the veggies. Start rolling, holding the filling in place as you make a tight roll; be sure to tuck in sides near the beginning. Roll all the way up and set on a platter. Repeat until all ingredients are used.

Whisk together sauce ingredients until well combined.

blissful variation

Use the *peanut sauce*, on page 82, for a dipping sauce.

chinese cabbage roll-ups • 82

chinese cabbage roll-ups

G 45 • Makes 6 servings

These are like the lettuce wraps I've had at Chinese restaurants. You can use lettuce or cabbage for the outside roll and your favorite veggie fillings.

1 tablespoon sesame oil
1 cup carrots, julienne
1 cup zucchini, julienne
1 cup green cabbage, julienne (save big outside leaves for roll-ups)
1 garlic clove, minced (optional)
1 teaspoon fresh ginger, minced
6 mushrooms, sliced
2 tablespoons tamari
1 tablespoon cilantro, minced
1 cup soybean sprouts
6 large green cabbage leaves or lettuce leaves

In a large skillet, heat oil over medium flame. Stir-fry next six ingredients, adding one at a time in the order listed. Stir-fry until vegetables are bright and slightly crisp. Add tamari and cilantro; toss. Remove from heat, then stir in sprouts.

To assemble the wrap, fill cabbage or lettuce leaf and roll up, tucking in the bottom edge.

---

peanut sauce

G 45 • Makes about 1 cup

This is the perfect sauce to use for a soba noodle salad, as a dipping sauce for spring rolls, or as a sauce for stir-fried veggies. Add a bit more water and it's great as a salad dressing!

½ cup unsalted creamy peanut butter
¼ cup filtered water
2 tablespoons tamari
2 tablespoons brown rice vinegar
1 tablespoon maple or brown rice syrup
Pinch red pepper flakes (optional)

Whisk together all the ingredients or blend in a blender until well combined.

---

quick and easy nachos

45 • Makes 2 to 3 servings

Nachos are one of my all-time favorite comfort foods or junk foods, but this version is far healthier. If you want to make it super healthy, use the oil-free nacho cheeze sauce *(recipe follows) rather than Daiya cheese. If you do this, skip the first step of melting the cheese in the oven.*

And speaking of the sauce... you will be pleasantly surprised at how cheesy and delicious this sauce is without the guilt of regular cheese. My recipe tester warns to be careful not to eat the whole thing in one sitting, or you'll get a tummy-ache. You've been warned!

2 handfuls tortilla chips (I like unsalted blue corn chips)
1 package Daiya cheese shreds or *oil-free nacho cheeze sauce* (recipe follows)
1 can (15 ounces) of your favorite vegan chili
1 cup cherry tomatoes, halved
Soy sour cream (optional)
Fire-roasted salsa (optional)
Green onions, chopped, for garnish

Preheat oven to 300 degrees F. Place tortilla chips in an ovenproof dish or baking sheet and sprinkle Daiya cheese all over. Bake for 12 minutes, or until cheese melts. While that is baking, make *easy guacamole*, on page 65.

Warm up vegan chili on the stovetop until hot. When the chips are done, spread them out on a plate and top with chili and fresh tomatoes. Serve with generous piles of *easy guacamole*, soy sour cream, and a side of fire-roasted salsa. Garnish with green onions.

oil-free nacho cheeze sauce

Makes about 1 cup

½ cup cashews, soaked 3 hours
⅓ cup slivered almonds, soaked 3 hours
5 tablespoons nutritional yeast
1 to 2 tablespoons lemon juice
1 tablespoon tamari
1 tablespoon arrowroot
½ cup unsweetened rice milk
Dash black pepper
Dash coriander
Dash paprika
Dash turmeric
Dash cayenne (optional for a spicy cheeze)

Drain nuts. In a food processor, combine all ingredients and blend until smooth. Be sure to scrape down the edges of the bowl a few times to incorporate all the ingredients. Season to taste if you want it saltier. Cook in a small saucepan over a low flame until it thickens and heats through, stirring continuously.

blissful suggestion

Drizzle on top of nachos, use as a dipping sauce or a topping for steamed veggies.

traditional miso

G ◊ 45 • Makes 4 to 5 servings

This is the most healing and traditional way of making miso soup. I like to include a root vegetable or two and a leafy green vegetable for added flavor and nutrients.

5 cups filtered water
1 to 2 tablespoons wakame, cut into small pieces
1 to 2 dried shiitake mushrooms
½ cup daikon, small dice
⅓ cup carrot, diced
1 cup leafy green of your choice: kale, Napa cabbage, collard greens, etc.
1 to 2 tablespoons barley miso

In a saucepan, bring water, wakame, mushrooms, and veggies to a boil. Reduce heat and simmer for about five to ten minutes. Remove mushrooms and allow to cool to the touch. Cut off woody stem and discard. Slice the caps into thin strips and put back into soup. Turn off flame. In a small bowl or tea cup, mix miso together with about ¼ cup of the soup broth until well dissolved. Stir back into the pot and let sit for a few minutes. Stir well and serve.

blissful tip

If it needs to be saltier for you, instead of adding more miso, which can be expensive, you can add a pinch of sea salt.

easy cheezy broccoli soup

G S ◊ 45 • Makes 4 to 6 servings

Broccoli and cheese just go so well together. But since I don't eat cheese anymore I use nutritional yeast for this great anytime soup.

1 tablespoon oil or ½ cup water
1 cup onion, diced
2 cups Yukon gold potato, cubed
Pinch sea salt
1 tablespoon dried basil
⅓ cup nutritional yeast
3 cups broccoli, chopped
5 cups filtered water
2 bay leaves
6 ounce carton unsweetened plain soy yogurt
Sea salt, to taste
Fresh basil, chiffonade for garnish

Heat oil or water in a stockpot over medium high flame. Sauté onion and potato with pinch of salt for two minutes covered. Add basil and nutritional yeast and sauté two more minutes. Add water if potatoes begin to stick. Stir in broccoli, water, and bay leaves and bring to a boil. Cover and simmer over low flame until potatoes are tender, about ten minutes. Remove bay leaves and cool slightly.

Puree soup in batches in a blender and return to pot. Stir in yogurt and heat over medium flame. Season to taste. Garnish with fresh basil and serve hot (for how to chiffonade your basil, see cutting tips on page 27). You also can serve this soup with a dollop of *cashew-garlic aioli*, on page 156.

"If we make our goal to live a life of compassion and unconditional love, then the world will indeed become a garden where all kinds of flowers can bloom and grow."

— Elisabeth Kubler-Ross

not-your-average fresh salads and dressings

When we switch to a plant-based diet, others often assume that all we eat is salads. While I love me some salad, it's not the only thing we plant-lovers eat. But If I had to eat only salads, I'd be perfectly content munching on these for a lifetime. Yes, they are *that* good. And salads are not just for chicks either. Munch on that.

spring

summer

autumn

winter

anytime

spring

spring kale salad with sweet miso dressing

[icons] G [icon] 45 • Makes 5 to 7 servings • **FAN FAVE**

If you've been scared to try kale raw, this salad is for you! This is the tastiest way I've ever had raw kale. You are sure to fall in love with this salad, as many people have before.

2 bunches kale, washed
1 cup cherry tomatoes, sliced in half
1 small fennel bulb, thinly sliced
2 avocados, cubed
2 tablespoons dulse flakes, for garnish

sweet miso dressing

1 lemon, zested and juiced
2 tablespoons yellow or white miso
2 tablespoons stone-ground mustard
2 tablespoons maple or brown rice syrup
2 tablespoons nutritional yeast
Salt and black pepper, to taste
Filtered water, as necessary

Pull leaves from stalk of kale and tear into small pieces. Thinly slice the stalk. Place in a medium bowl. Blend dressing ingredients together in blender or by hand until smooth. Massage the kale with dressing for about five minutes. Stir in the rest of salad ingredients and allow to sit for 15 minutes, while the flavors meld.

---

goddess mint dressing

G 45 • Makes about 1 cup

I haven't tasted many tahini-based dressings that I've liked, so I made up my own. Paired with mint and the perfect amount of sweetness, this is sure to be a hit.

3 tablespoons tahini
3 tablespoons apple cider vinegar
2 tablespoons tamari
2 tablespoons maple or brown rice syrup
2 tablespoons lemon juice
¼ cup fresh mint
Filtered water, as necessary

Blend all ingredients except filtered water in blender or food processor. Add water as needed to get the consistency you desire. Refrigerate up to one week.

creamy basil dressing • 89

creamy basil dressing

  • Makes about 2 cups

This is like pesto, but it's a dressing.

⅓ cup cashews, soaked 3 hours
⅓ cup pine nuts, washed
1 cup basil, packed
1 tablespoon white miso
2 tablespoons balsamic vinegar
1 tablespoon lemon juice
½ teaspoon sea salt
Pinch black pepper
Filtered water, as necessary

Drain nuts. Combine all ingredients except filtered water in food processor and blend until well combined and no lumps remain. Add filtered water to get the consistency you prefer. Refrigerate up to one week.

lemon-miso dressing

G 45 • Makes about ½ cup

Lemons are high in vitamin C, which helps neutralize free radicals. Miso has vitamin B12, protein, and a world of health benefits. Pair these two and you've got a pretty special salad dressing that's good for your health!

¼ cup lemon juice
2 tablespoons flax oil (optional)
2 teaspoons white miso
2 teaspoons maple syrup, or more to taste
1 to 1½ tablespoons tahini, roasted preferred
1 tablespoon soy sauce or tamari
1 tablespoon brown rice vinegar or apple cider vinegar
Sea salt and black pepper, to taste

Mix all ingredients in a blender or whisk by hand in a small bowl until smooth. Refrigerate up to one week.

summer

avocado, strawberry, and grape tomato salad

• Makes 2 to 4 servings

Strawberries are the most popular berry in the world. They go great in salads and are a complement to a savory vinaigrette dressing—like the balsamic vinaigrette, *on page 102, in this recipe.*

1 avocado, cubed
1 small carrot, thin matchsticks
7 grape tomatoes, halved
4 strawberries, thick slices
½ cup yellow pepper, thinly sliced
6 butter lettuce leaves, washed and torn
Pinch black pepper and sea salt
***Balsamic vinaigrette*, page 102**

Toss salad ingredients together in a medium bowl with the amount of vinaigrette you prefer. Serve immediately.

summer fruity kale salad

G S 45 • Makes 3 to 5 servings

In case you can't get enough raw kale variations, this one is perfect for summer, when strawberries are at their peak. Jicama is a Mexican root vegetable that is light, crispy, and perfect for summer, too.

4 cups packed kale, off the stem and torn into small pieces
1 tablespoon walnut oil
1 tablespoon balsamic vinegar
½ teaspoon sea salt
2 cups jicama, peeled and cut into matchsticks
1 cup strawberries, sliced
1 tablespoon maple syrup
2 tablespoons fresh mint, chopped
3 tablespoons dried coconut flakes
1 tablespoon lime juice
½ cup raisins

Place the first four ingredients in a large bowl and massage the kale with your hands for about five minutes. Stir in the rest of the ingredients until well combined. Let sit for 15 minutes to let flavors meld.

blissful tip: diversify

The most important thing you can do is have a varied diet rich in natural, whole foods. Eat foods in all the colors of the rainbow. Kale, lettuce, and celery for green; carrots, yams, and oranges for orange; eggplant for purple; cabbage, strawberries, and apples for red; pineapple, squash, and grains for yellow; grapefruit for pink; beans for brown; cauliflower, daikon, and tofu for white. You get the picture. Fruits and vegetables that are beautifully colored are rich in antioxidant elements that protect us from free radicals. Start by adding things like whole grains and more vegetables. Then you can start slowly taking things away that aren't serving your greater good. This book shows you how to do this, and you know what? You might just find a fountain of youth. A balanced, whole food, plant-based diet can give you the energy and nutritional support to make your body, mind, and spirit happy.

zucchini "pasta" with mint-cashew pesto sauce • 92

zucchini "pasta" with mint-cashew pesto sauce

[icons] G 45 • Makes 3 to 5 servings • **CHEF FAVE**

This is one of my favorite raw vegan dishes and one that friends always love. You can make "noodles" out of carrots, cabbage, daikon, and summer squash with a gadget called a Spiralizer, or try the method described below. Give them all a try with this delicious mint pesto.

2 medium zucchini, washed and made into pasta

mint-cashew pesto sauce

makes about 1½ cups

1 cup fresh mint
1 cup fresh parsley
1 cup cashews, soaked 2 to 4 hours, then drained
½ cup nutritional yeast
2 tablespoons tamari
1 tablespoon apple cider vinegar
1 tablespoon maple or brown rice syrup
Pinch sea salt and black pepper
2 tablespoons or more filtered water, as necessary to get creamy texture

Combine all pesto ingredients in a food processor and blend until smooth. Be sure to scrape the edges of the bowl a few times to incorporate all the ingredients.

To make zucchini noodles without a Spiralizer, take a peeler and run it across the zucchini length-wise. Continue to do this, moving around the zucchini so one piece of noodle isn't wider than the others. Keep going until you reach the very seedy part of the zucchini. Discard.

Toss zucchini pasta with a dollop of pesto. Add as much pesto as you'd like to pasta. Serve cold.

raw pasta with almond sauce

• Makes 4 to 6 servings

Kelp noodles are one of my favorite products in the world. Raw, light, cooling, and delicious, when they're paired with a rich almond sauce, you get a heavenly pasta dish without the guilt of eating high-carb pasta.

1 package kelp noodles, drained
1 cup carrot, thin matchsticks
1 cup cucumber, halved, seeded, and thinly sliced
½ lime, squeezed on top at the end of preparation
Cilantro, for garnish

almond sauce

1 cup almonds and ¼ cup sunflower seeds, washed and soaked 3 hours
2 tablespoons tamari
3 tablespoons apple cider vinegar
1 tablespoon maple syrup
1 teaspoon toasted sesame oil (optional)
2 tablespoons miso
1 tablespoon dulse flakes
Filtered water, as needed

Drain nuts and seeds. In food processor, combine all the sauce ingredients except the filtered water and blend until well combined. Be sure to scrape the edges of the bowl a few times to incorporate all the ingredients. Add water as needed to get the consistency you prefer. Toss desired amount of sauce with the rest of pasta ingredients; garnish with cilantro and a squeeze of lime.

blissful definition

Dulse is a red-colored sea vegetable that is high in trace minerals. It often comes in flakes, either in a bag or in a spice shaker.

---

cilantro-lime dressing

• Makes about 1 cup

If you want an oil-free dressing that is still rich and satisfying, try this one. The pumpkin seeds give it a rich flavor, while the cucumbers make it light and fluffy.

2 tablespoons pumpkin seeds, washed and drained
2 tablespoons nutritional yeast
1 cup cilantro, tightly packed
1 lime, zested and juiced
2 tablespoons tamari
1 garlic clove (optional)
1 tablespoon maple syrup
1 cup cucumber, chopped

Blend in a blender until well combined and no chunks remain. Refrigerate for three to five days.

arugula-edamame salad with orange-sesame vinaigrette • 95

autumn

arugula-edamame salad with orange-sesame vinaigrette

G 💧 45 • Makes 3 to 4 servings

This bright, happy salad is quick and easy with a Chinese flair. The spiciness of the arugula goes perfectly with the tartness of the oranges.

1 cup shelled edamame
3 cups arugula or 1 bag of pre-washed arugula
1 red bell pepper, thinly sliced
1 can (11 ounces) mandarin oranges, drained and washed
Toasted sliced almonds, for garnish

orange-sesame vinaigrette

1 orange, zested and juiced
1 tablespoon tamari
1 tablespoon maple syrup
1 tablespoon brown rice vinegar
1 teaspoon toasted sesame oil
Pinch black pepper

Cook edamame according to the package instructions. Drain and rinse with cold water. Combine with all other salad ingredients except almonds in a bowl. Whisk together dressing ingredients in a small bowl. Toss with salad or serve separately. Garnish with almonds.

fall harvest fruit salad

G S 💧 45 • Makes 5 to 7 servings

There are plenty of fruits available during the fall season, so enjoy them with this delectable fruit salad! Serve alone, or with your morning oatmeal or cereal.

1 small cantaloupe (about 4 cups), peeled, seeded, and cubed
1 apple, cored and sliced
1 cup red grapes, washed and halved
2 clementines, peeled and sliced (or 1 navel orange)
1 lemon, zested and juiced
¼ cup dried grated coconut
½ cup pecan halves

Combine all ingredients in a medium bowl. Keep refrigerated up to one day.

blissful suggestion

Also great with *key-lime soy yogurt* and *coconut bliss granola*, on page 35.

fall harvest fruit salad • 95

open sesame dressing

G ♢ 45 • Makes about 2 cups

This will give ranch dressing a run for its money! So rich and luscious, this dressing can be used as a dip for crudités, on a salad, or in a sandwich or wrap.

1 package Mori Nu silken tofu
1 teaspoon arrowroot
1 teaspoon toasted sesame oil
3 tablespoons brown rice or sherry vinegar
2 tablespoons white or yellow miso
1 clove garlic, sliced (optional)
1 green onion, minced
2 tablespoons brown rice or maple syrup
Filtered water, as needed
Sea salt, to taste
1 tablespoon sesame seeds, toasted

Blend all ingredients except the sesame seeds in a blender until smooth. Add water to get your desired consistency. Season with sea salt as necessary. Add toasted sesame seeds and transfer to a glass jar with lid or an old dressing container. Refrigerate up to one week and shake well before each use.

---

sweet pumpkin dressing

G S ♢ 45 • Makes about 1 cup

This is a great autumn dressing that can be made with any hard squash, but I prefer kabocha, butternut, or pumpkin.

1 cup cooked pumpkin or squash
½ cup water, or more to desired consistency
2 tablespoons sweetener
2 tablespoons avocado
Sea salt, to taste

Blend all ingredients until well combined and no chunks remain. Season with sea salt and add water to get your desired consistency. Serve with fresh salad.

winter

apple salsa

 • Makes about 1½ cups

A great way to use apples in season, this salsa is full of antioxidants, fiber, and flavonoids, which help keep LDL cholesterol in check. Try it served inside a wrap or with tortilla chips.

2 Granny Smith apples, cored and small cubes
Handful cilantro, leaves removed from stem
1 tablespoon lime juice
1 tablespoon orange zest
1 tablespoon tamari
1 tablespoon mirin
1 tablespoon brown rice or maple syrup
Dash cayenne (optional for a kick)

Combine all ingredients in a small bowl. Allow to marinate for 15 minutes while flavors meld.

---

blood orange and fennel salad with sweet mustard dressing

G S 45 • Makes 5 to 7 servings

This salad is one of my favorites, because the spiciness of the fennel pairs so brilliantly with the sweet mustard dressing. I soak the veggies in the dressing to absorb the flavors and create a quick pickle effect.

1 cup fennel, thinly sliced
1 red bell pepper, cored and thinly sliced
¼ red onion, thinly sliced (optional)
2 blood oranges, peeled and sliced into wedges
1 head leafy lettuce, washed and torn into pieces
1 avocado, cubed
1 cup walnuts, chopped and toasted

sweet mustard dressing

1 teaspoon grapeseed oil
3 tablespoons maple syrup
¼ cup Dijon mustard
2 tablespoons sherry wine or red wine vinegar
Pinch black pepper
Sea salt, to taste

Blend all dressing ingredients in a small bowl until well combined. Soak fennel, red bell pepper, and onion, if using, in a bowl with dressing for 30 minutes, tossing occasionally.

Place lettuce, orange slices, and avocado in a serving bowl. Pull veggies out of dressing and toss with lettuce mix. Sprinkle walnuts on salad and serve immediately.

ginger-miso dressing • 99

mac n' kale salad • 100

balsamic vinaigrette

G S 45 • Makes about ½ cup

This is like traditional balsamic vinaigrette only healthier and with less oil. I like my balsamic dressings a little bit on the sweet side, but you can use less maple syrup if you prefer it more savory.

1 tablespoon olive oil
¼ cup balsamic vinegar
1 teaspoon lemon zest
Pinch sea salt and black pepper
¼ cup lemon juice
2 to 3 teaspoons maple or brown rice syrup
1 clove fresh garlic, sliced (optional)
Sea salt, to taste

Blend dressing ingredients in a blender or whisk by hand. Add sea salt to taste. Refrigerate up to one week.

blissed caesar dressing

G 45 • Makes about 1 cup

Most bottled caesar dressings are not vegan because they either have cheese or anchovy paste in them. This is a healthier version that is not full of oil. It's made with high-quality ingredients that do not feel heavy.

2 tablespoons almonds, soaked 2 hours
2 tablespoons pumpkin seeds, soaked 2 hours
1 clove garlic (optional)
2 tablespoons nutritional yeast
2 tablespoons tamari
1 small lemon, zested and juiced
3 tablespoons Dijon mustard
1 tablespoon maple syrup
¼ cup water, as needed
1 tablespoon flax seed oil (optional)
Sea salt, to taste

Drain almonds and pumpkin seeds. Grind almonds in food processor for a minute. Add remaining ingredients and blend until smooth. Be sure to scrape down the edges of the bowl a few times to incorporate all the ingredients. Season with sea salt if necessary.

"Enchant, stay beautiful and graceful, but do this, eat well. Bring the same consideration to the preparation of your food as you devote to your appearance. Let your dinner be a poem, like your dress."

— Charles Pierre Monselet, French author
Letters to Emily

delectable vegetable sides

Vegetables are a staple of the plant-based diet. I encourage you to gorge on them and fill half your plate with veggies in all the colors of the rainbow. They are packed with the micronutrients, vitamins, and minerals we need for good health and longevity. In this chapter, I'll explain the different methods for cooking vegetables and give you delicious recipes that will never leave you bored. If you let the seasons dictate which vegetable you use, each recipe can be transformed into a new dish as the year goes on, offering unlimited possibilities.

spring

summer

autumn

winter

anytime

cooking techniques for veggies

stir-frying/sautéing

These are basically the same thing. But there are two different ways to sauté explained below. The trick to the perfect stir-fry/sauté is how you cut each vegetable and knowing the timing of when each veggie goes into the skillet. The thicker you cut the vegetable, the longer it will take to cook. A root vegetable is going to take longer than a water-dense or green veggie, such as cabbage or kale. The most important first step is that the skillet be hot, so when the veggies go in, they start to sizzle immediately. This will lock in the flavor and nutrients.

oil sautéing

This is the most common way to do a sauté. You need a large enough skillet to allow room for the veggies to move around. Heat the skillet with oil (how much depends on recipe) over medium/high flame. Do not let the oil smoke, but you want the skillet to be hot when the first vegetable goes in. You can test one piece to see if it sizzles. When hot, lovingly place the veggie that requires the longest cooking time (usually the hardest/thickest) into the oil with a pinch of sea salt. This adds flavor and moves along the cooking process. Stir the veggies around until well coated with oil and shake the pan back and forth to prevent sticking. This is when I turn the flame down to about medium. Add in the next vegetable and stir it around. Sometimes I will put a lid on so the veggies steam and cook faster, or I put a touch of water in the pan if the vegetables begin to stick. Continue adding veggies. This is when you'll stir in any dried spices for a dish. The most water-dense vegetable will go in last. Depending on the vegetable and how thin you cut it, it may not need to cook for more than a minute. Remove from heat to a platter or bowl to help slow down the cooking process so the veggies stay crisp.

Depending on how many veggies and the cutting styles of each, this process should take no more than 10 minutes.

water sautéing

Water sauté is the same process as the oil sauté, but it's a healthier, lower-fat way of cooking. Just know that the veggies will not taste as rich. Instead of oil, I coat the bottom of the skillet with about one-third to one-half cup of water or broth. When it begins to sizzle, I put the veggies inside in the same order as above.

blanching/boiling

This is hands-down my favorite way of cooking vegetables. Blanching is a technique of submerging vegetables into boiling water. The type of veggie, its freshness, and how you cut it (shape and thickness) will determine how long it stays in the water. It's quick and easy, and the process allows the vegetables to hold on to almost all their nutrients. It's good any time of the year and helps you stay hydrated. Your pot size will be determined by how many vegetables you plan on cooking at one time. If it's just a small amount for you or one other, a small pot will be fine. You really don't need to fill it all the way, either. Leafy greens are going to shrink considerably in size, so there is no point in wasting water. You are going to need your skimmer for this.

Bring a small, medium, or large pot with two inches of water to a rolling boil with a tiny pinch of salt. Submerge your vegetable (least bitter and lighter in color first) into the boiling water. Allow the veggies to bubble around for about 15 seconds for water-dense veggies and up to 45 seconds for harder vegetables. I personally like my vegetables just tender and not overcooked. Never walk away from the pot. You can usually tell it's time to pull them from the water when the color of the vegetable gets really bright. It sort of yells at you, "I'm ready, pull me out!" Keep in mind that unless you shock them with cold water after you pull them out, the veggies will continue to cook. Often I will run cold water over the veggies just to make sure they don't overcook, or I pull them out very quickly from the boiling water. Boiling is when you leave the vegetable in longer and cover with a lid. Root vegetables like squash and sweet potato need more time and need to be boiled.

steaming

I use the steaming method to warm up food more than using it as a regular technique. I prefer to blanch/boil veggies because I feel like you are less likely to overcook them. There's some debate as to whether steaming holds the most nutrients in the vegetable. Try both ways and see which you like the most. To steam, get a small, medium, or large pot, depending on how much you are going to steam at one time. Ideally you want to have only one layer of veggies inside the steamer basket to make sure that nothing gets undercooked. You only need a small amount of water in the pot; just enough as to not go above the steamer basket. Bring to a boil, cover with a lid, and set a timer. The time depends on the vegetables, the size, shape, and thickness you cut the vegetables. Most veggies should take no more than five minutes.

roasting/baking

I love roasting and baking vegetables during the colder months of the year. It's so warming and comforting. Certain veggies, like root vegetables, are just made to be roasted. You can do it two ways. Cut in chunks or cubes and toss with a little olive oil, sea salt, and spices. Or you can cook them *sans* oil by placing the veggies in a casserole dish with sea salt and a tiny amount of water in the bottom, cover, and bake. As with any cooking method, cooking time depends on the thickness of the vegetable and the way you cut it. The trick to getting all your veggies to cook evenly is to cut the heartier veggies smaller than the water-dense veggies.

grilling

Yes, there is a place for grilling in plant-based cooking! The grill is not just for meat, poultry, or fish. I like to marinate veggies, tofu, and tempeh before I put them on the hot grill. Also brush the marinade over the vegetables while they cook. This is a quick style of cooking, which makes it perfect for summer, but not so good for heartier root veggies. Stick with things that cook fast, like water-dense summer vegetables.

stewing and braising

These are two cooking methods that I don't use often, living in Southern California, but they are great for colder weather or when we are feeling weak. Braising is typically cooking one type of vegetable slowly in a small amount of stock or water. The veggies release their juices, creating a burst of rich flavor. Stewing is cooking different types of veggies slowly by cutting them into chunks, bringing them to a boil, and simmering on a low flame, covered. Stir occasionally.

frying

This is something I rarely do, even though fried foods sure taste good! If you are eating a healthy plant-based diet, having something fried every once in a while is not going to kill you. You just won't find many recipes in this book that use this technique. Actually, only two; *lotus root chips*, on page 124, and the *tempeh "fish" tacos* on page 194 have the option for frying. I use the shallow frying technique, which involves using a frying pan with about one-fourth to one-half inch of oil in the pan. Heat oil over medium/high heat before adding the vegetables. When you put the veggies in the pan, they should sizzle and jump around. Cook on both sides until crispy, then drain on a paper towel.

african collard stir-fry • 110

spring

african collard stir-fry

G ⧫ 45 • Makes 3 to 5 servings

I love Southern comfort-style collard greens, but most of the time the dish is full of oil and fat, and the greens are cooked until there is no life left in them. This is my healthier, more vibrant version with a touch of orange.

½ cup water
2 cups sweet potatoes, matchsticks
Pinch sea salt
⅓ cup orange juice
1 tablespoon peanut butter
2 tablespoons tamari
½ teaspoon curry powder
½ cup carrot, matchsticks
2 tablespoons raisins (optional)
1 bunch collards, stems removed, leaves in chiffonade (page 27), 4 stems thinly sliced on diagonal

Heat water in a medium skillet. When water boils, add sweet potato and sea salt, cover with lid, and simmer for three to five minutes. Meanwhile, whisk together juice, peanut butter, tamari, and curry. Add carrots, raisins, and collards with sauce mix in skillet. Simmer for three to five minutes, until all the veggies are tender but not mushy. Stir occasionally to coat the greens with the sauce.

burdock, squash, and brussels stir-fry

G S 45 • Makes 3 to 5 servings

You may have seen burdock at the grocery store, but didn't pick it up because it looks like tree bark. It's surprisingly tasty and good for your blood. Give this recipe a whirl and you'll be pleasantly surprised by the unique flavor combination.

1 tablespoon sesame oil
2 cups butternut squash, peeled and small cube
½ cup burdock, matchsticks
Pinch sea salt
Filtered water, as needed
9 Brussels sprouts, trimmed and quartered

Heat oil in skillet over medium flame. Add squash and burdock with a pinch of salt and sauté for about five minutes, covered. Stir occasionally and add a little water as needed if veggies begin to stick. Add Brussels sprouts and a bit of water. Cover and sauté for three more minutes, stirring occasionally.

dijon dill green beans • 113

lemon-roasted asparagus • 112

lemon-roasted asparagus

G S 45 • Makes 3 to 5 servings

Fresh lemon is paired with asparagus and fresh oregano for a spring or summer side dish. Since it cooks so quickly, your oven won't need to be on for long.

1 pound fresh asparagus, woody ends trimmed
2 tablespoons lemon, sliced very thin, seeds removed
1 tablespoon olive oil
2 tablespoons fresh oregano, chopped
½ teaspoon fennel seeds
½ teaspoon sea salt
½ teaspoon black pepper

Preheat oven to 450 degrees F. Combine all the ingredients in a medium bowl, making sure to completely coat all the asparagus spears with oil. Spread out evenly on a rimmed baking sheet. Roast, shaking the pan occasionally to toss, until the asparagus is tender-crisp, about 12 minutes.

dijon dill green beans

G 45 • Makes 4 to 6 servings

This recipe is so quick, easy, and delicious that you'll want to add it to your quick dinner repertoire. Green beans are low in calories and contain a long list of vitamins and minerals. Pair them with dijon dill dressing *and almonds, and you've got yourself a pretty nutritious side!*

1 pound green beans, washed and trimmed
1 cup sliced almonds, washed and toasted

dijon dill dressing

makes about ½ cup

¼ cup olive oil
2 tablespoons red wine vinegar
2 tablespoons lemon zest
2 tablespoons lemon juice
2 tablespoons Dijon mustard
2 tablespoons maple syrup
½ teaspoon sea salt
½ teaspoon black pepper
1 tablespoon tahini
1 tablespoon white miso
1 tablespoon fresh dill

Fill a medium-size pot with about 3 inches of water and bring to a boil. Blend dressing ingredients in a blender or whisk in a small bowl. Add green beans to boiling water, return to a boil, and remove within 45 seconds. Drain beans, toss with dressing, and garnish with sliced almonds.

green spring casserole

45 • Makes 5 to 7 servings

I created this recipe with the many fresh greens that are available during the spring. It makes a great side dish with any meal. To make this casserole gluten-free, look for gluten-free breadcrumbs at the natural food store, make your own, or just leave them out.

¼ cup vegetable broth
1 teaspoon cumin seeds
1 bunch dinosaur (lacinato) kale, chiffonade (page 27)
7 large cremini mushrooms, sliced
¼ cup unsweetened almond milk
1 tablespoon Dijon mustard
2 tablespoons tamari
2 tablespoons nutritional yeast
2 cups green beans, ends trimmed, cut into 1-inch pieces
1 cup panko breadcrumbs (optional)

Preheat oven to 350 degrees F. Heat broth in a skillet. Sauté cumin seeds for a few minutes, then stir in kale and mushrooms and cover with lid. Let veggies cook for a few minutes. Meanwhile, stir together the milk, mustard, tamari, and yeast in a small bowl. Stir sauce and green beans into the kale mixture. Simmer for three minutes, stirring occasionally. Transfer veggies to a casserole dish, top with panko breadcrumbs and bake uncovered for 12 minutes.

summer

lemon-basil potato salad

G 45 • Makes 8 to 10 servings

As the warm weather approaches, it's time to break out the picnic basket and the BBQ grill. This fresh take on potato salad uses a light basil dressing instead of heart-clogging mayonnaise, and is great to take to your next picnic in the park. Feel free to halve this recipe if you aren't feeding a ton of people.

2 cups green beans, trimmed and cut into 1-inch pieces
Filtered water
4 pounds red potatoes, scrubbed and cubed
½ cup red onion (optional)
Pinch sea salt and black pepper

lemon-basil dressing

1 cup fresh basil, tightly packed and chopped
1 tablespoon olive oil
3 tablespoons balsamic vinegar
1 tablespoon Dijon mustard
2 tablespoons tamari
1 lemon, zested and juiced
½ cup vegan mayonnaise (optional)
Sea salt, to taste

Bring a large pot of water to a boil. Blanch green beans until tender. Pull out with skimmer and drain, keeping cooking liquid in pot. Place potatoes in same pot and bring back to a boil. Add pinch of sea salt and black pepper and simmer until potatoes are almost tender. Do not overcook!

While potatoes are cooking, mix the dressing ingredients together. Drain potatoes in a colander, splashing with cold water to prevent overcooking. Toss potatoes, green beans, red onion (if using), and dressing together. Add sea salt as needed.

---

magical raw tacos

G 45 • Makes 3 to 5 servings • **FAN FAVE**

The spread can make a lot *of tacos, so feel free to cut the recipe in half, or keep in the fridge for up to five days. Once you taste these suckers, you'll understand why they are called "magical"!*

1 head romaine lettuce, washed
1 medium carrot, thin matchsticks
1 cup cucumber, diced small

1 avocado, cubed small
6 basil leaves, chiffonade (page 27)

red pepper-cashew spread

makes about 2 cups

1 cup cashews, soaked 3 hours
2 tablespoons tamari
1 tablespoon maple syrup
1 tablespoon apple cider vinegar
1 lemon, zested and juiced
1 cup red bell pepper, chopped
Pinch sea salt
Cayenne (if you want it spicy)

For the spread, drain cashews. In a food processor, blend the first five ingredients together until fairly creamy, about one minute. Add the rest of spread ingredients and blend until smooth, about two minutes. Be sure to scrape down the edges of the bowl to incorporate all the ingredients.

To assemble tacos, spread *red pepper-cashew spread* on a lettuce leaf and top with a sprinkle of carrot, cucumber, avocado, and basil. Repeat for each taco. Serve immediately.

wasabi sweet potato salad • 116

wasabi sweet potato salad

G 45 • Makes 5 to 7 servings

This is my version of a favorite salad found at a macrobiotic restaurant in Los Angeles. Feel free to adjust the amount of wasabi to your liking. A little usually goes a long way, though!

3 white sweet potatoes, washed and cubed (about 4 to 5 cups)
1 cup Persian cucumbers, diced
½ cup carrots, grated
½ cup vegan mayonnaise
Pinch sea salt and black pepper
2 tablespoons Dijon mustard
1 tablespoon brown rice vinegar
1 teaspoon wasabi paste, or more for spicier dish
Sea salt, to taste

Steam (page 107) sweet potatoes until just tender. Allow to cool, then toss with cucumbers and carrot in a medium bowl. Whisk together the rest of the ingredients in a small bowl, then fold into veggies. Add sea salt as needed. Refrigerate for 15 minutes before serving.

nishime (waterless cooking)

G · S · 45 • Makes 3 to 5 servings

This is a traditional Japanese cooking method that uses a small amount of water to slowly cook vegetables until they release their juices. Root veggies work best, but be creative and try whichever vegetables strike your fancy.

1 inch-piece dried kombu, soaked one minute
1 medium rutabaga, cut into thick diagonal slices
6-inch piece daikon, cut into thick rounds
2 medium carrots, cut into 2-inch "logs"
2 medium parsnips, cut into thick diagonal slices
Filtered water
½ teaspoon tamari

Cut the kombu into little squares. In a heavy pot with a lid, spread the squares of kombu along the bottom. Layer the rutabaga, daikon, carrots, and parsnips respectively. Pour roughly ¼ to ½ inch of filtered water into the pot. Cover and bring to a boil. Reduce heat and let simmer 15 to 20 minutes, or until parsnips are soft. Season with tamari and simmer five more minutes.

---

southwest grilled corn salad with cilantro-lime dressing

G · S · 45 • Makes 5 to 7 servings

This will be your new favorite summer picnic and BBQ dish. It's great paired with black beans and served over salad greens.

7 ears fresh corn, shucked
2 bell peppers (your choice of color), roasted whole on grill, five minutes, rotating frequently
2 small zucchini, sliced in half, roasted on grill, three minutes each side

cilantro-lime dressing

¼ cup olive oil
1 cup cilantro, tightly packed
2 limes, zested and juice
2 tablespoons maple or brown rice syrup
Pinch sea salt and black pepper

Roast corn on the grill at medium heat for eight minutes, turning frequently. Cool, then cut kernels from cob and place in a medium bowl. When peppers and zucchini have cooled, dice and combine with corn.

Blend dressing ingredients in blender until smooth. Toss with salad ingredients. Allow 15 minutes for flavors to blend.

blissful variation

Add hot sauce to the dressing for a kick!

blissful suggestion

If you don't have a grill, you can roast the corn in the oven at 375 degrees F for about 30 minutes, turning occasionally. The peppers and zucchini will take about 10 to 20 minutes.

lemon-kissed brussels and butternut squash • 119

autumn

lemon-kissed brussels and butternut squash

G · [oil-free] · 45 • Makes 4 to 6 servings • **CHEF FAVE**

I know so many people who think they don't like Brussels sprouts, but after trying this dish, they realize they just haven't had them cooked well. If you think you are a Brussels hater, try this dish immediately!

3 cups butternut squash, peeled and cut in ½-inch cubes
2 cups Brussels sprouts, halved, ends trimmed
⅓ cup slivered almonds
1 teaspoon ginger, grated
1 tablespoon lemon zest
1 tablespoon lemon juice
1 tablespoon tamari
1 tablespoon maple or brown rice syrup
1 tablespoon brown rice vinegar (or other vinegar)
Sea salt, to taste

Steam butternut squash until just tender. Place in a medium bowl. Steam Brussels sprouts until just tender and place in bowl with squash. Pan-toast almonds in a skillet over a medium-low flame until golden brown, stirring continuously. Mix together the rest of the ingredients in a small bowl, then toss with veggies and almonds until well combined. Season with sea salt to taste.

---

pumpkin with apricot-ginger glaze

G · [oil-free] · 45 • Makes 4 to 6 servings

Kabocha is hands-down my favorite winter squash. When paired with the sweet and spicy ginger glaze, it's heavenly. If you can't find kabocha you can substitute peeled butternut squash.

Filtered water (enough to line the pot to a 1-inch depth)
1 small kabocha squash, seeds removed and cubed (about 2 cups)
Tamari
⅓ cup red bell pepper, thinly sliced
Cilantro, for garnish

apricot-ginger glaze

1 tablespoon tamari
1 tablespoon brown rice or maple syrup
1-inch piece ginger, minced
2 tablespoons apricot preserves

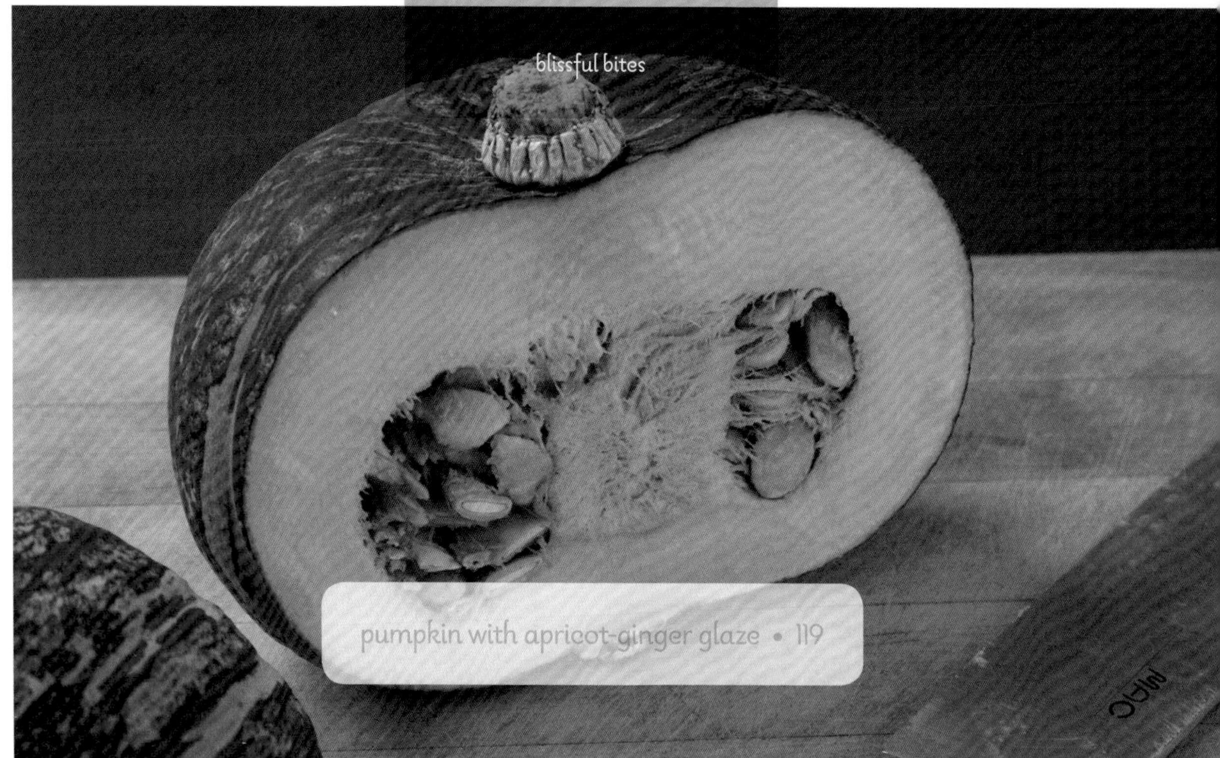

pumpkin with apricot-ginger glaze • 119

Steam squash. Sprinkle lightly with soy sauce before covering with lid. Steam until tender. Test one piece with a fork at around seven minutes. You want the squash soft and tender but not mushy. Meanwhile, mix together glaze ingredients.

Remove squash from steamer basket and place in a medium bowl. Toss with the rest of ingredients and glaze. Serve hot or cold. Garnish with cilantro.

---

root fries

G S • Makes 3 to 4 servings

If you love French fries, this is a light version using naturally sweet root vegetables. I bake them instead of frying because it's healthier and uses less oil.

1 large jewel yam, washed and scrubbed
1 small rutabaga, washed and scrubbed
1 medium carrot, washed and scrubbed
1 medium parsnip, washed and scrubbed
Extra virgin olive oil (or coconut oil)
Pinch sea salt and black pepper
Optional spices: basil, rosemary, oregano, cumin, coriander, curry powder, or cinnamon

Preheat oven to 400 degrees F. Cut veggies into thin French-fry-sized sticks. Place on baking sheet and mix in olive oil, pepper, sea salt, and spices, until the sticks are well coated.

Bake for 30 minutes, then toss. Continue baking until brown or crispy, about 45 minutes total (or if you like them soft, cook for 40 minutes).

root fries • 120

kale salad with curry-coconut sauce

G 45 • Makes 3 to 4 servings

This is a great way to serve greens. The dressing is good on soba noodles as well—or you could make this into a noodle bowl.

1 medium carrot, cut on the diagonal
3 red radishes, thinly sliced
1 bunch kale, chopped
½ cup arame, washed and soaked five minutes

curry coconut sauce

makes about 1 cup

1 tablespoon curry powder
½ cup light coconut milk
¼ cup unsalted, unsweetened peanut butter
1 tablespoon maple or brown rice syrup
3 tablespoons yellow or white miso
Filtered water, as necessary
Pinch red pepper flakes (optional)

Blanch veggies (see cooking tips on page 107). Drain arame and veggies, then toss together in a medium bowl. Blend the sauce ingredients in a blender until smooth. Toss as much as you like with the vegetables and arame. Sauce will keep refrigerated for three days.

sweet potato puree

G S 45 • Makes 4 to 6 servings

This is a delicious side dish that most everyone will love. It's a lovely combination of sweetness and spice that has many health benefits. The cinnamon regulates your blood sugar level and is known to reduce LDL cholesterol.

2 garnet yams, peeled and cubed
Pinch sea salt
Filtered water
½ tablespoon ground coriander
1 teaspoon orange zest
2 tablespoons balsamic vinegar
½ teaspoon cinnamon
Dash of nutmeg
Sea salt, to taste

Put yams and pinch of sea salt in medium saucepan with enough water to cover and bring to a boil. Simmer with the lid on for 20 minutes, until yams are very tender. Drain and return to saucepan. Mash yams with remaining ingredients with hand masher or in food processor. Stir well. Add sea salt as needed.

fried lotus chips • 124

winter

fried lotus chips

G S 45 • Makes 3 to 5 servings

This is one of only two recipes you'll find in this book that is fried. These lotus root chips are a perfect substitute for potato chips and are a great snack for kids and adults alike. Lotus root can be found at any Japanese market and many natural food stores.

5-inch piece lotus root
Safflower or sesame oil

Slice the lotus root into very thin rounds. Coat the bottom of a cast-iron skillet with oil and heat over medium-high flame. When the oil is hot, delicately place the lotus root slices in the pan and fry for one to two minutes. Flip and fry on other side until golden brown and crispy. Drain on paper towel, then serve.

lemon-roasted beets, brussels, and yams

G S • Makes 5 to 7 servings

This is a divine dish, but you must make sure that the beet slices don't touch the other veggies because beets turn everything that they touch red!

2 cups Brussels sprouts, ends trimmed and cut in quarters
1 medium yam, ½ inch matchsticks
1 small lemon, zested and juiced
⅛ cup olive oil
Generous pinch sea salt
Dash black pepper
1 large beet, peeled, halved, and thinly sliced
¼ cup parsley, chopped, for garnish
⅓ cup pumpkin seeds, toasted

Preheat oven to 400 degrees F. Mix the first six ingredients together in a large bowl, making sure all vegetables are coated well with oil. Transfer to a baking dish or sheet, placing veggies on one half of the sheet. Put the beet in the same bowl and toss to coat with oil. Place beet slices on the other side of the baking sheet. Bake for one hour, or until beets are tender. Check on the veggies and toss at 30 minutes. Place in a serving dish and toss with parsley. Sprinkle pumpkin seeds on top. Serve immediately.

gingery bok choi-burdock sauté • 125

gingery bok choy-burdock sauté

  45 • Makes 2 to 4 servings

This is a Japanese-style stir-fry that has no oil but tons of protein and health benefits. Ginger has many anti-inflammatory properties, while chickpeas are full of fiber and folate for blood sugar regulation.

⅓ cup water
Pinch sea salt
1 cup burdock, cut thinly on the diagonal
1 teaspoon ginger, grated
1 bunch bok choy, chopped, greens separated
1 cup cooked chickpeas, or 1 can (15 ounces), drained and rinsed
1 tablespoon tamari, or more to taste
Sea salt, to taste

Bring water to a boil in medium skillet with a lid. Place burdock in water and simmer covered with a pinch of sea salt until almost tender, about four minutes. Stir in ginger and bok choy stalks; cover, and steam for three minutes, stirring occasionally. Add bok choy greens, chickpeas, and tamari; cover and steam for two more minutes. Add sea salt as needed.

miso-baked daikon

G ⓞ 45 • Makes 3 to 4 servings

Daikon is a foreign vegetable to most people, but the Japanese have eaten it for eons. It's a bit spicy, but the longer you cook daikon, the sweeter it gets. It's good for pulling excess fat and dairy from the body and is usually served grated alongside dishes like tempura.

3 cups daikon, cut into ½-inch half-moons
Pinch sea salt
2 tablespoons yellow or white miso
1 tablespoon mirin
Parsley, chopped for garnish

Boil daikon with a pinch of sea salt for 10 minutes. Reserve ¼ cup of cooking water and mix with miso and mirin for the sauce. Drain daikon, mix with miso sauce, and place in casserole dish. Bake 25 minutes at 350 degrees F, tossing occasionally. Garnish with parsley.

perfect winter stew

G S • Makes 4 to 6 servings

There's nothing like a warm, comforting stew on a cold day. This one is filled with good-quality sweet vegetables like yams and winter squash, along with other vegetables. It's a nutrient-packed one-pot meal.

1 tablespoon safflower oil
2 garnet yams, small chunks
½ kabocha squash, seeded and small chunks
Pinch sea salt
1 tablespoon cumin
½ teaspoon cinnamon
1 teaspoon marjoram
1 teaspoon grated ginger
1 carton No-Chicken Broth
2 cups filtered water
2 celery stalks, cut on the diagonal
8 mushrooms, sliced
1 can (15 ounces) kidney beans, drained and rinsed
Dash cayenne (optional, if you like a kick)
Sea salt, to taste

Heat oil in a soup pot. Sauté yams and squash with pinch of salt for a few minutes. Add cumin, cinnamon, and marjoram, and coat veggies well. Add ginger, broth, water, and sea salt, and bring to a boil. Simmer covered for 25 minutes, stirring occasionally. Add celery, mushrooms, and beans, and simmer uncovered for another 20 minutes, stirring occasionally. Season with cayenne, if using, and sea salt to taste.

anytime

asian green bean stir-fry

• Makes 4 to 6 servings

This is a simple, light and lovely dish that has a zingy Asian sauce everyone will love.

1½ pounds green beans, ends trimmed, cut into 2-inch pieces
2 cups cremini mushrooms, ends trimmed and sliced
Toasted sesame seeds, for garnish

asian dressing

1 teaspoon grated ginger
2 tablespoons tamari
1 tablespoon mirin
2 tablespoons maple syrup
1 teaspoon toasted sesame oil

Blanch (see page 107) green beans until just tender. Mix together dressing ingredients. In a medium skillet, sauté green beans and mushrooms with dressing. Simmer, stirring occasionally, about five minutes until green beans are heated through and mushrooms are cooked. Garnish with toasted sesame seeds.

basil-cashew cheeze sauce

G 45 • Makes about 3 cups

This makes the most delicious pizza topping, pasta sauce, steamed veggie sauce, or wrap sauce. You won't miss the oil or the cholesterol you get with real cheese!

1½ cups raw cashews, soaked 1 hour
1 package Mori Nu silken tofu
1 cup basil, chopped
½ cup nutritional yeast
2 tablespoons white or yellow miso
2 tablespoons tamari
1 lemon, juiced
1 tablespoon apple cider vinegar
Nondairy milk, as needed

Drain cashews and blend with tofu in food processor until the mixture is finely ground but not a paste. Add the rest of ingredients and process until smooth, making sure to scrape down the edges of the bowl occasionally. If you would like a thinner sauce, add nondairy milk as needed.

basil-cashew cheeze sauce • 127
fire-roasted tomato sauce • 129

blanched greens with basil-pecan pesto sauce

G O 45 • Makes 3 to 4 servings

This is a tasty way to get your greens and calcium. The pesto sauce makes a great topping for any vegetable dish and can also be served with pasta or as a sauce for pizza.

1 bunch kale, washed and chopped
1 cup sugar snap peas, tips removed
Filtered water

basil-pecan pesto sauce

makes about 1 cup

½ cup pecans, toasted
2 cups packed basil
2 tablespoons white miso
1 tablespoon maple syrup
2 tablespoons balsamic vinegar
1 lemon, zested and juiced
Filtered water, as necessary
Sea salt, to taste

Blanch (see page 107) the kale and snap peas until lightly cooked. Meanwhile, blend pesto ingredients in a food processor, adding water as necessary to obtain the desired consistency. Be sure to scrape down the edges of the bowl to incorporate all the ingredients. Add sea salt and pepper as needed. Drain veggies and serve with a dollop of pesto.

fire-roasted tomato sauce

G O 45 • Makes about 2 cups

This sauce is great for many things. I like to use it as pizza sauce, as a dipping sauce for the sage-infused polenta fries, *on page 155, or as a pasta sauce.*

1 can (28 ounces) fire-roasted tomatoes
1 tablespoon tamari
1 tablespoon balsamic vinegar
2 tablespoons nutritional yeast
1 teaspoon dried basil
½ teaspoon dried oregano
½ teaspoon marjoram
½ teaspoon thyme
Dash black pepper

Combine all ingredients in a medium saucepan. Heat over a medium flame and simmer until ingredients are well combined and heated through, about five minutes.

---

tropical relish

G S O 45 • Makes about 4 cups

This tropical relish is a great topping for grains, salads, and sandwiches, and is good served with crackers, too. This recipe makes quite a lot, so feel free to halve it. Mangoes are full of vitamins and minerals, protecting you against heart disease and other ailments, while basil is a powerful herb that strengthens your cells.

1½ cups ripe mangoes, peeled, pitted, and finely chopped
½ cup red bell pepper, finely chopped

1 cup fresh basil, chopped
1 cup tomato, finely chopped
1 tablespoon balsamic vinegar
Dash lime juice
Pinch sea salt and black pepper

Mix all ingredients in a bowl and allow flavors to meld for 15 to 30 minutes.

blissful suggestion

Serve this with the *marinated portobella steaks*, recipe below.

---

marinated portabella steaks

G S • Makes 4 servings

These portabella steaks are exactly as they sound: like steak. They are great to serve to heavy meat-eaters because the portabella mushroom, once seasoned and marinated, has a similar texture to steak, but without the saturated fat. These are great on a sandwich or in a wrap, sliced on top of a salad, made into fajitas, or served at your next BBQ party.

4 portabella mushrooms, stems cut off and wiped with damp paper towel

marinade

¼ cup red wine vinegar
2 tablespoons balsamic vinegar
2 tablespoons olive oil
1 lime, juiced
2 tablespoons maple syrup
1 tablespoon Dijon mustard
Pinch sea salt and black pepper

Place marinade ingredients in a plastic bag and shake to blend. Add mushrooms, coat with marinade, and refrigerate for one hour. Grill mushrooms directly on hot grill for a few minutes on each side.

blissful variation

Add fresh herbs such as rosemary or thyme to the marinade.

If you don't have a grill, bake the portabellas at 350 degrees F for eight minutes, turning once.

marinated portabella steaks with tropical relish • 130 and 129

broccoli salad with creamy mustard dressing • 132

broccoli salad with creamy mustard dressing

G 45 • Makes 3 to 5 servings

This is a healthy plant-based take on salads you may have had at a salad bar or at potlucks. It is easy to make and will be a crowd-pleaser at get-togethers. It's also a great way to use leftover beans. If you throw in some cooked quinoa, it makes a one-pot meal perfect to take to work for lunch.

1 large crown broccoli, cut into florets
1 large carrot, grated
1 cup cooked chickpeas, or 1 can (15 ounces), drained and rinsed
2 red radishes, thinly sliced

creamy mustard dressing

½ cup vegan mayonnaise
2 tablespoons Dijon mustard
1 tablespoon maple syrup
1 tablespoon sherry or apple cider vinegar
Pinch sea salt and black pepper

Steam the broccoli until crisp-tender, about two minutes. Remove from heat and toss with rest of salad ingredients. Whisk together dressing ingredients in small bowl. Toss with salad and chill for 10 minutes before serving. Great the next day!

"Health is a state of complete harmony of the body, mind, and spirit. When one is free from physical disabilities and mental distractions, the gates of the soul open."

— B.K.S. Iyengar

whole grains and carbs do a body good

A grain a day will keep the doctor away. Wait, that's not right, but it should be. We need whole grains in our lives! Grains can be stored for thousands of years, transported across many seas, and feed billions of people. They are close to the perfect food and have been eaten by traditional cultures for ages. Grains supply the complex carbohydrates that our bodies need for brain function, blood-sugar regulation, and metabolism stabilization, and they help keep our digestive tracts running smoothly, all while keeping us centered—allowing us to connect to our bliss.

spring

summer

autumn

winter

anytime

a grain for every occasion

Not all grains are created equal. There are whole grains, cracked grains, and grain products, and then there are refined grains from which you want to stay far away. The USDA daily recommendation for grains is three to five servings, with half of those being from *whole* grains. What they fail to mention is that most of the "whole" grains that we eat tend to not be whole at all. A whole grain has the bran, germ, and endosperm still intact. So bread or flour is not a whole grain. Not that you can't eat bread every once in a while, but most of your complex carbohydrates should be actual whole grains. Their health benefits are immense. Whole grains are excellent at sustaining blood sugar, supplying good fiber to keep everything running smoothly, giving you lasting energy, and lowering cholesterol, and are full of many beneficial vitamins and minerals. Below are some of my fave grains.

rice

There are endless types of rice: brown rice is the staple grain and comes in short, medium, long, basmati, and jasmine. The first two are for daily use; the last three I tend to eat in warmer months because they are light and cook quickly. Then there are fancier rice varieties, such as black forbidden, Bhutanese red, Arborio, and wild rice. Use different kinds of rice to add variety to your cooking.

quinoa

Quinoa is actually a seed, but it gets thrown in the whole grain section. It's probably my favorite grain next to Lundberg's "Golden Rose" medium brown rice. It has the highest amount of protein of all the grains and is one of your best sources of plant-based protein. So have your fill! It's great for warmer months because of its quick cooking time.

millet

Millet is the most underappreciated of the grains and is usually associated with bird food. It is naturally sweet, making it great for the pancreas and those with blood sugar disorders. It's good all year round and is excellent in soups, for soft grain dishes, paired with sweet vegetables, or used as a base for burgers and croquettes.

barley

Barley is one of those grains you either love or you don't. It is hearty, and its energy is known for being relaxing. It's great mixed with other grains and in soups. Be sure to get hulled barley, rather than pearled barley, which has been stripped of its fiber and minerals. My favorite barley-esque grain is *hato mugi*. It may be hard

to find, and can be quite expensive since it comes from East Asia, but once you try it, you will know why it's my favorite. The taste and texture is unlike any other grain I've tried.

corn

Yes, corn is a grain! It's naturally sweet and delicious. It's been getting a bad rap lately since it's one of the highest GMO crops and is used to make nasty products like high fructose corn syrup. If you can get it organic, local, and non-GMO, I think it's great to have in the summer when it's usually grown. The cracked grain *polenta*, or *corn grits*, is found in this cookbook, which is easier to digest than corn, and nourishing to the heart.

oats

Rarely does anyone actually eat whole oats anymore. The oats you probably know are steel-cut or rolled oats. These are more of a cracked-grain than whole, but don't worry. You get some of the benefits that oats give; high in protein, minerals, vitamins, and cholesterol-lowering fiber.

buckwheat

I rarely eat buckwheat as a whole grain, but I love eating soba noodles as an alternative that adds variety to my diet. Noodles are grain products, and I eat them on occasion. Using buckwheat flour adds a new dimension to baked goods.

wheat

We all know what wheat is, but most of our wheat comes in the form of flour, bread, crackers, cereals, and seitan. Ideally, if you are eating these grain products, make sure they are made with whole wheat and whole grains, rather than enriched or refined grains. If you have a gluten intolerance, you can try the many gluten-free breads that are now available at any natural food store. Wheat berries, the actual whole-wheat grain, is hearty and mixes well with brown rice.

spelt

Spelt is becoming a popular grain to use as flour in breads and desserts. It's naturally wheat-free but does have gluten in it.

teff/amaranth

These are the tiniest grains. They make the perfect breakfast porridge, and they mix well with other grains. They are high in calcium and protein, and have a rich, nutty flavor.

other cracked grains and grain products

Whole-grain pastas are great to have on occasion or when you need to make something quickly. I really love brown rice and quinoa pasta, which are both gluten-free and available at any natural food store. Couscous and bulgur are also grain products that require very little preparation time. These are not whole grains, so you want to eat them sparingly and not as your sole source of complex carbohydrates.

grain basics

to soak or not to soak

Like most things in the cooking world, there are differing opinions on whether soaking grains is good or unnecessary. One thing you must always do is wash the grains. In my opinion, some grains do need to be soaked for better digestion and taste. Three to six hours is fine, or overnight. Short- and medium-grain brown rice, barley, and whole oats do best with soaking.

to salt or not to salt

With most grains, I use a pinch of salt. Everyone's pinch is different, so grab a few grains of salt between your thumb and your forefinger. Don't go crazy with the salt. It's one pinch per cup of grain. If I'm pressure-cooking brown rice, instead of salt I like to use kombu (a sea vegetable explained on page 166).

combining grains

For added variety and flavor, try experimenting with different grain combinations in the same pot. If they have a fairly similar cooking time, they can be combined. I usually stick with two grains at the most, and you can do 80/20, 60/40, or 50/50. It's delicious to add other things to your grains, like chestnuts or other nuts, beans, or root veggies, so get creative with those grain dishes!

dry-roasting

Some grains, particularly millet, taste magnificent when dry-roasted in a skillet before cooking. To see how this is done, see the *asian quinoa and millet pilaf* recipe, on page 149.

barley "hato mugi" pilaf • 141

spring

barley "hato mugi" pilaf

  • Makes 4 to 6 servings

Hato mugi is my favorite grain, but it's very expensive and hard to find. Feel free to substitute barley for this recipe if you can't get a hold of hato mugi.

1 cup hato mugi
½ cup vegetable broth
2 cups butternut squash, peeled and cubed
Pinch sea salt
1 tablespoon coriander
Dash paprika
2 tablespoons mirin
6 big leaves fresh basil, chopped

Cook hato mugi according to package instructions. Meanwhile, heat broth in a medium skillet with butternut squash and pinch of sea salt. Cover and simmer for five minutes, stirring occasionally. Add spices and mirin, and simmer until squash is tender. If it begins to stick, add a touch more broth. When hato mugi is done, combine with squash and basil in a medium bowl. Serve warm or cold the next day.

blissful mediterranean salad

 • Makes 4 to 6 servings

This is a great salad for warmer weather and will make you feel like you're in Greece. Not that I've ever been to Greece, but I feel like I'm in sitting on an island overlooking the water when I have this salad.

1½ cups Israeli couscous
¼ cup filtered water for sautéing
6 sun-dried tomatoes (not in oil), soaked in hot water for 10 minutes, sliced
2 cups zucchini, cut in half-moons
1 cup fresh corn, off the cob
1 tablespoon tarragon
1 tablespoon thyme
2 tablespoons balsamic vinegar
2 tablespoons tamari
1 can (4 ounces) chopped olives, or ½ cup fresh chopped olives
1 teaspoon olive oil
½ cup cherry tomatoes, halved
Sea salt and black pepper, to taste

Cook couscous according to the package directions. Meanwhile, heat water in a medium skillet and water sauté zucchini and corn with the spices for a few minutes. Stir in vinegar, tamari, and olives and set aside. Toss couscous with olive oil, veggie mixture, and both sun-dried and cherry tomatoes. Let sit for 15 minutes to allow the flavors to meld. Season with sea salt and black pepper as needed. Great served cold.

not-your-usual pad thai

G 45 • Makes 5 to 7 servings

This is not your usual pad thai...as the name states. I love pad thai, but I also really love Thai curry, so I came up with a sauce that is a fusion of my two favorite Thai dishes to create this. Don't try to compare it to the pad thai you've had in the past; just appreciate it for its uniqueness.

pad thai sauce

½ teaspoon red chili paste (or more for spiciness)
½ cup raw sliced almonds
¼ cup fruit-sweetened apricot jam
2 tablespoons dulse
2 tablespoons tamari
1 lime, zested and juiced
1 teaspoon ginger, minced
2 tablespoons white miso
½ cup water

1 package (8 ounces) rice noodles
1 medium zucchini, half-moon
1 medium carrot, matchsticks
1 cup cilantro leaves
2 cups bean sprouts
1 cup cucumbers, matchsticks
1 lime, juiced, for garnish

Blend *pad thai sauce* ingredients in a food processor until well combined and no chunks remain. Meanwhile, cook rice noodles according to package and lightly steam zucchini and carrots. Toss veggies, noodles, and sauce in a medium bowl with cilantro, sprouts, and cucumbers. Let sit for 10 minutes to let flavors meld. Garnish with a dash of lime juice.

blissful variation

If you want your sauce to be spicier feel free to add more chili paste.

quinoa tabouli

G S 45 • Makes 6 to 8 servings

This recipe is a different take on traditional tabouli, usually made with bulgur wheat. Quinoa is the highest protein grain available, which makes it a better choice. This tabouli will be even better the next day!

1 cup quinoa, rinsed
1⅓ cups filtered water
Pinch sea salt and black pepper
3 Persian cucumbers, diced
1 large tomato, chopped (or 1 cup cherry tomatoes, halved)
⅓ cup dried apricots
Handful chopped mint and parsley, to taste
1 teaspoon coriander
1 teaspoon cumin
1 small lemon, zested and juiced
1 small lime, zested and juiced
Red wine vinegar, to taste
Dash olive oil
Season to taste

Place quinoa, water, and pinch of sea salt in a medium pot and bring to a boil. Cover, reduce

quinoa tabouli • 142

to simmer, and cook for 20 minutes. Fluff with a fork, then place in a large bowl and fold in the rest of ingredients. Let sit for 15 minutes to let flavors meld. Season with sea salt as needed.

---

simple lemon-scented basmati rice

G S ◊ 45 • Makes 4 to 6 servings

This rice dish is simple and fast and reminds me of a rice dish served at Casa de Luz, my favorite macrobiotic café in Austin, Texas.

1 cup brown basmati rice, washed and drained
2 cups filtered water
Pinch sea salt
2 teaspoons lemon zest
1 tablespoon lemon juice
1 bay leaf
1 cup frozen peas, defrosted
2 tablespoons finely chopped fresh parsley
¼ cup pumpkin seeds, toasted

In a medium saucepan, combine the first six ingredients. Bring to a boil, cover, and simmer for 40 minutes, or until all water has been absorbed. Turn heat off, and let rice sit, undisturbed for five minutes. Stir in peas and parsley gently with a fork and remove bay leaf. Serve garnished with pumpkin seeds.

summer

basic polenta

 • Makes 4 to 6 servings

This is the basic way to make polenta, which is a light summer grain. You can add different kinds of spices to customize polenta to go with any meal.

1 cup polenta, washed
3 cups filtered water or broth
Pinch sea salt
Spices of your choice

Combine ingredients in medium pot. Heat over medium flame. When polenta begins to bubble, turn flame to low and whisk continuously. Polenta will start to thicken. Continue to whisk over low flame until whisk stands up on its own and polenta begins to pull away from the pot. This could take about 10 to 15 minutes. Pour into casserole dish and allow to cool, then slice. Or serve immediately if you like the porridge texture.

blissful variation

After the polenta sets, cut into 1-inch slices and pan-fry until golden brown on both sides.

blissful suggestion

Make a napoleon by layering polenta slices with blanched vegetables and *fire-roasted tomato sauce*, on page 129 drizzled with *basil-cashew cheeze sauce*, on page 127.

coconut polenta

G • 45 • Makes 6 to 8 servings

Polenta is often overlooked when we think of grains, but it's so versatile and quick to make. It can be served at any meal and goes great with blanched greens with basil-pecan pesto sauce, *on page 129, and a side of* basic beans, *on page 202.*

2 cups polenta, rinsed
2 cans (13½ ounces each) coconut milk
3 cups filtered water
1 tablespoon coriander
1 tablespoon umeboshi or red wine vinegar
2 tablespoons tamari
Pinch sea salt

Combine ingredients in medium pot. Heat over medium flame. When polenta begins to bubble, turn flame to low and whisk continuously. Polenta will start to thicken. Continue to whisk over low flame until whisk stands up on its own. Pour into casserole dish and allow to cool.

blissful variation

Add one teaspoon cinnamon and one tablespoon orange zest for a breakfast treat.

---

red quinoa salad

 • Makes 6 to 8 servings

One of my favorite cafés in Los Angeles has a similar quinoa salad that I love. I created my own with a touch of fresh basil and avocado–minus the oil.

1 cup quinoa, washed
1 teaspoon coriander
1 teaspoon oregano
Pinch sea salt
1½ cups filtered water
1 cup beets, peeled, cubed, and boiled
½ cup carrots, grated
⅓ cup fresh basil, chopped
1 tablespoon lemon zest
Pinch black pepper
2 tablespoons sherry vinegar
2 tablespoons tamari
1 avocado, diced
½ cup sunflower seeds, toasted

Place quinoa, dried herbs, salt, and water in a medium pot. Bring to a boil, then simmer for 20 minutes, covered. Lightly toss the rest of the ingredients, except avocado and seeds, in a medium bowl. When quinoa is done, fluff with a fork and stir into the other ingredients. Fold in avocado. Chill and serve garnished with sunflower seeds.

---

penne with creamy red pepper sauce

G 45 • Makes 4 to 6 servings

This is a big hit with kids and parents alike! It's a great quick meal when you don't feel like making a production for dinner. My recipe tester's husband thought it had goat cheese in it; it's that creamy and yummy!

1 package (16 ounces) brown rice penne pasta
1 tablespoon coconut oil
1 medium carrot, diced
3 cups red bell pepper, diced (2 to 3 peppers)
1 small garlic clove, minced (optional)
¼ cup fresh basil, chopped
1 package Mori Nu silken tofu
¼ cup nutritional yeast
1 tablespoon red wine vinegar
2 tablespoons tamari
Pinch black pepper
Sea salt, to taste

Cook pasta according to package instructions. Meanwhile, heat oil in skillet and sauté vegetables with garlic until soft, about five minutes. Stir in basil and remove from heat. Blend sautéed vegetables with the rest of ingredients in a blender or food processor. Add

fiesta quinoa salad • 146

sea salt to taste. Serve over penne or your favorite gluten-free pasta.

---

fiesta quinoa salad

G 45 • Makes 5 to 7 servings

This Mexican-inspired quinoa salad uses both regular and red quinoa for added texture and beauty. If you can't find red quinoa, you can use all white.

1 cup white quinoa, plus ¼ cup red quinoa, washed and drained
1 cup fresh corn, off the cob
2 cups filtered water
Pinch sea salt
1½ cups cooked black beans, or 1 can (15 ounces), rinsed and drained
¼ cup yellow pepper, finely diced
¼ cup tomatoes, diced
¼ cup cilantro leaves
Season to taste

dressing

2 teaspoons lime zest
2 tablespoons lime juice
2 teaspoons cumin
2 teaspoons chili powder
3 tablespoons tamari
1 tablespoons maple syrup
2 teaspoons apple cider vinegar

Place quinoa, corn, and water in a medium saucepan with pinch of sea salt and bring to a boil. Simmer covered for 20 minutes over low flame. Meanwhile, whisk the dressing ingredients in a small bowl until well combined. Fluff quinoa with a fork, place in medium bowl, and stir in the black beans, veggies, dressing, and cilantro. Season with sea salt if needed. Serve warm or cold the next day.

blissful tip: enjoy eating and cooking at home

Try to have meals at regular or scheduled times each day. Sit down with no distractions and chew your food well. We get most of our nutrients through the breakdown that happens in our mouth. That means if you don't chew your food, you aren't getting the vitamins and minerals you need from it. Slow down and enjoy the process of nourishing your body. And do not overstuff yourself! It's uncomfortable, and it taxes your digestive organs. If you can try to stay at 80 percent full, your body will feel light and full of energy. If you give your body too much food to process, energy needed elsewhere is diverted to aid in digestion.

Cook more meals at home. It costs less than going out to eat, creates less waste, and you'll know where your food is coming from and how it has been treated. By cooking your own food, you put your own qi or life force into it, making it alive with energy. Plus, most restaurants serve food prepared with poor quality oil, too much salt, and tons of sugar. Does that sound blissful to you?

sushi rice bowl

G (drop icon) 45 • Makes 4 to 6 servings • **CHEF FAVE**

This dish is like an open-faced sushi roll. A beautiful dish to take to a potluck or party.

1 cup long-grain brown rice, washed
1 cup Japanese cucumber, diced (or any cucumber will do)
½ cup frozen corn, defrosted (or fresh if in season)
½ cup frozen peas, defrosted
½ cup red bell pepper, finely diced
2 tablespoons dulse flakes
2 tablespoons brown rice vinegar
1 teaspoon toasted sesame oil
2 tablespoons tamari
2 tablespoons pickled ginger, minced
1 sheet nori, torn or cut into little strips
Butter lettuce
Toasted sesame seeds, for garnish
½ cup cilantro

Cook rice according to package instructions. While rice cooks, place all ingredients except lettuce, sesame seeds, and cilantro in a large bowl, then add rice and fold together. To serve, cover platter with lettuce leaves and spoon rice in the middle. Garnish with sesame seeds and cilantro.

autumn

asian millet and quinoa pilaf

   • Makes 6 to 8 servings

My two favorite grains are paired to make a grain dish with a touch of Asian flair that's good any time of the year. Roasting the grains first brings out their naturally sweet flavor.

1 cup millet, washed
½ cup quinoa, washed
Filtered water
Pinch sea salt
2 cups zucchini, cut in quarter-moons
1 cup shelled edamame
1 cup fresh corn, off the cob
1 tablespoon fresh ginger, grated
1 tablespoon mirin
1 tablespoon tamari
1 tablespoon brown rice or red wine vinegar
¼ cup pumpkin seeds, toasted
Handful cilantro leaves
Sea salt, to taste

Roast millet and quinoa in a large saucepan over medium-high flame, stirring continuously, until all the water is gone and grains get golden brown. Add 3⅓ cups water and salt and bring to a boil. Cover with lid and reduce to a low flame. Simmer for 20 to 25 minutes. Fluff with a fork.

Meanwhile, in ¼ cup filtered water, water sauté the zucchini, edamame, and corn in a separate pan with ginger, mirin, tamari, and brown rice vinegar until the veggies are tender but still crisp, about four minutes. Fold veggies into the millet-quinoa mixture and toss with pumpkin seeds and cilantro. Season with sea salt as needed.

---

millet mashed "potatoes"

45 • Makes 5 to 7 servings

This recipe turns millet into a creamy mashed potato-like dish, without the refined carbs of potatoes. Give this version a try and you'll be surprised how much it tastes and feels like real mashed potatoes!

1 cup millet, washed
4 cups water or broth
2 cups cauliflower, in small florets
Pinch sea salt
1 tablespoon tahini
Black pepper and sea salt, to taste
Parsley, for garnish

Place all ingredients in a saucepan except parsley, cover, and bring to a boil. Reduce to medium-low and simmer 25 to 30 minutes. Remove from flame and mash with potato masher. Season to taste.

mushroom gravy

Makes about 4 cups

You are going to flip about how yummy, rich, and savory this gravy is; yet, it's the healthiest version ever. My recipe tester thought it was so amazing that it could be bottled as a Christmas gift!

2 tablespoons safflower oil
½ onion, diced (optional)
8 mushrooms, stems removed and sliced
1 teaspoon dried sage
1 teaspoon thyme
1 teaspoon black pepper
Pinch sea salt
4 cups vegetable stock
2 tablespoons tamari or soy sauce
2 tablespoons balsamic vinegar
½ cup nutritional yeast
½ cup barley flour (or other whole-grain flour), plus additional flour as needed
2 tablespoons white miso, dissolved in ½ cup stock
Parsley, for garnish

Heat oil in large pot. Sauté onion, if using, with a pinch of sea salt until translucent, about two minutes. Stir in mushrooms. Add spices and sauté another two minutes. Add 3½ cups of the stock, tamari, and vinegar. Slowly add in nutritional yeast and flour, stirring continuously with a whisk to prevent lumping. Add the remaining stock and miso while whisking. Simmer until gravy thickens, about 15 minutes.

Taste and adjust sea salt and spices as needed. Add more flour gradually to get the thickness you prefer.

To serve, spoon a mound of millet on plate, top with gravy and garnish with parsley.

macro "mac and cheeze"

G 💧 45 • Makes 6 to 8 servings • **FAN FAVE**

This is a healthier take on traditional mac 'n' cheese, made with wholesome ingredients— no fake cheese or heavy oil. You'll be surprised at how similar it tastes while it leaves you feeling light and happy. My recipe tester loved this so much she wrote a song about it!

4 cups butternut squash, peeled, seeded, and cubed
1 teaspoon tamari
2 boxes (8 ounces each) quinoa pasta shells
1 package Mori Nu silken tofu
2 tablespoons white miso
2 tablespoons tahini
1 small lemon, juiced
2 tablespoons tamari
¼ cup nutritional yeast
Dash black pepper
Paprika, for garnish

Steam squash until tender, splashing tamari on before covering with lid. Meanwhile, boil the pasta according to instructions on the box. When squash is tender, blend with the rest of ingredients, except pasta and paprika, in a food processor until smooth. Be sure to scrape down the edges of the bowl to incorporate all the ingredients. Toss sauce with pasta and bake in a casserole dish at 350 degrees F for 15 minutes. Remove from oven and sprinkle with paprika for garnish. Serve immediately.

macro "mac and cheeze" • 150

pressure-cooked brown rice • 153

pressure-cooked brown rice

G S [icon] • Makes 5 to 7 servings

This is my favorite way to prepare brown rice because pressure cooking makes the grain sweet and flavorful. Depending on your climate, it may not be the best way to cook grains, but give it a try. Lundberg medium "Golden Rose" is my favorite brown rice ever!

1 cup medium-grain brown rice, washed and soaked four to six hours
1¼ cups filtered water
1-inch strip kombu or pinch sea salt

Drain rice. Place new filtered water, rice, and kombu in the pressure cooker. Lock lid in place and heat over medium flame. When up to pressure place flame deflector (if you have one) underneath the pot and simmer on low flame for 45 minutes. You want the flame low enough to keep the dial up to pressure, but not so high that there is heavy steam coming out of the top. Turn off flame and allow pressure to come down naturally. Or release dial if in a hurry. Fluff with a rice paddle and stir in kombu or sea salt.

not-so-forbidden rice salad • 155

winter

not-so-forbidden rice salad

  45 • Makes 5 to 7 servings

I love black rice because it's quick-cooking and has a unique taste profile. Feel free to change up the veggies and spices to make your own unique dish for each season.

1 cup black forbidden rice, washed
1¾ cups plus ½ cup filtered water
Pinch sea salt
2 cups sweet potatoes, small cube
1 teaspoon tarragon
1 teaspoon coriander
Dash black pepper
2 tablespoons sherry vinegar
1 tablespoon tamari
⅓ cup packed basil, chiffonade (page 27)
Sea salt, to taste

Place rice, 1¾ cups filtered water, and a pinch of sea salt in a medium saucepan and bring to a boil. Cover and reduce flame to a simmer for 30 minutes. Meanwhile, heat ½ cup water in a medium skillet. When it begins to sizzle, add sweet potatoes, a pinch of sea salt, and spices to the skillet and combine well. Cover and let simmer for about five minutes. Add a touch more water if it's sticking and stir in the remaining ingredients except basil. Cover and cook for another three minutes.

When rice is done, place in a medium bowl with the veggie mixture. Fold in all the ingredients until well combined. Season with sea salt, as needed.

---

sage-infused polenta fries

G S • Makes 5 to 7 servings

These are a great healthy substitute for fatty french fries and go great with cashew-garlic aioli, *on page 156,* fire-roasted tomato sauce, *on page 129, or* basil-cashew cheeze sauce, *on page 127.*

Oil spray, for casserole dish and baking sheet
1 recipe for *basic polenta*, on page 144
2 tablespoons fresh sage
2 tablespoons nutritional yeast
¼ teaspoon paprika
⅛ teaspoon nutmeg
¼ teaspoon coriander
Sea salt and black pepper, to taste

Combine additional ingredients, except sea salt and black pepper, in the pot with polenta and follow the directions in the *basic polenta* recipe, on page 144. Lightly spray medium casserole dish with oil. You want a dish that will make the polenta about ½ inch thick (about 9x13). Pour

sage-infused polenta fries with cashew-garlic aioli • 155 and 156

polenta inside and smooth over evenly. Let sit for 45 minutes until it hardens.

Preheat oven to 400 degrees F. Carefully flip the polenta out onto a cutting board and slice into french-fry shapes. Spray a baking sheet with oil, place fries about ¼ inch apart, sprinkle sea salt and pepper on top, then spray lightly with oil. Bake for 15 minutes, then flip and bake another 20 minutes or more, depending on how crunchy you want them.

cashew-garlic aioli

G S 💧 45 • Makes about ¼ cup

This vegan sauce is great for sandwiches, wraps, and as a dipping sauce for fries.

2 tablespoons raw cashews, soaked 1 hour
2 tablespoons sesame seeds
1 teaspoon garlic

3 tablespoons coconut milk
½ tablespoon coconut oil
1 tablespoon lime juice
Sea salt, to taste

Drain cashews. Combine all ingredients in a blender and blend until well combined, about two minutes. Season with sea salt to your preference.

---

tofu ricotta cheeze

G ♢ 45 • Makes about 2 cups

This is the best substitute for cheese in lasagna or pasta shells, spreading on pizza, or even inside a wrap.

1 package (14 ounces) extra firm tofu
⅓ cup fresh basil
½ cup nutritional yeast
2 tablespoons tamari
1 tablespoon red wine vinegar
1 tablespoon lemon juice
1 teaspoon maple syrup
1 cup fresh arugula or spinach
Pinch black pepper
Sea salt, to taste

Blend all ingredients except sea salt in a food processor until well combined and no lumps remain, about four minutes. Be sure to scrape down the edges of the bowl to incorporate all the ingredients. Season with sea salt and process again for a minute.

wild harvest pilaf

G S ♢ 45 • Makes 7 to 8 servings

Around the holidays you may be looking for a delicious and beautiful dish to serve in addition to traditional stuffing or in place of; this is that dish! I use a Lundberg wild rice blend, but feel free to use a mix of whatever rice you have along with wild rice.

2 cups wild rice blend, rinsed and drained
3 cups filtered water
½ cup orange juice
Pinch of sea salt
1 tablespoon orange zest
⅓ cup orange juice
¼ cup dried cranberries
¼ teaspoon cinnamon
1 teaspoon oregano
1 teaspoon coriander
¼ cup toasted pine nuts
⅓ cup parsley, chopped
Sea salt, to taste

Bring first four ingredients to a boil in a medium saucepan. Cover with lid and lower flame to a simmer. Cook for 40 minutes, or until rice is done. Fluff and place in a medium bowl. In a small saucepan, combine the rest of ingredients except nuts and parsley. Heat over a medium flame for a few minutes. Fold mixture into the rice with nuts and parsley. Season with sea salt and serve immediately.

veggie-stuffed pasta shells with mama mia magnifico sauce • 159

veggie-stuffed pasta shells

Makes 5 to 7 servings

This is going to be a favorite in your house, especially if you've recently dumped dairy and miss lasagna.

1 package (16 ounces) large/giant pasta shells
1 teaspoon oil
1 cup zucchini, diced small
1 cup mushrooms, finely chopped
***tofu ricotta cheeze*, on page 157**
***mama mia magnifico sauce*, recipe below**

Cook pasta according to package instructions. Heat oil in medium skillet, then sauté zucchini and mushroom until barely limp. Turn off heat, then mix in *tofu ricotta cheeze*, on page 157. Stuff filling into the pasta shells, then cover with *mama mia magnifico sauce* (recipe follows).

---

mama mia magnifico sauce

G ◬ 45 • Makes about 6 cups sauce

This is an amazing spaghetti sauce made without nightshade tomatoes that I learned how to make at The Natural Epicurean. This is great for those trying to stay away from nightshades because of joint problems. You would never know this isn't made with tomatoes! Great to use with pasta, lasagna, sloppy joes, or any other time you need a tomato base, like with BBQ sauce or ketchup.

1 medium butternut squash, peeled, seeded, and cut into large chunks
1 medium rutabaga, quartered
3 medium carrots, cut in large chunks
Filtered water
½ teaspoon sea salt
1 tablespoon oil
3 celery stalks, diced
½ cup onion, diced
1 tablespoon dried basil
1 tablespoon dried oregano
1 teaspoon dried thyme
1 tablespoon umeboshi vinegar (or sherry vinegar)
1 tablespoon balsamic vinegar
2 tablespoons tamari
1 tablespoon maple syrup
1 small beet, grated
Sea salt, to taste

Place squash, rutabaga, and carrots in a pressure cooker with water half the height of the vegetables. Add ½ teaspoon sea salt, lock lid in place, and bring up to pressure. Cook at full pressure for 15 minutes. Meanwhile, heat oil in skillet over medium flame and sauté celery, onion, spices and a pinch of sea salt for a few minutes. Stir in umeboshi vinegar, balsamic vinegar, tamari, and maple syrup, then set aside.

When root vegetables are done, turn off flame and let pressure come down naturally. Remove lid. When vegetables have slightly cooled, puree in a food processor or blender. Fold in sautéed celery, onion, and grated beet. Add as much beet as necessary to make the sauce a deep red. Season to taste with sea salt and black pepper. Warm over medium flame until hot and serve over pasta.

anytime

brown rice: boiled method

  • Makes 5 to 7 servings

If you live in warmer climates, the boiling method is best to use. It's a lighter cooking method than the contractiveness of pressure-cooking.

1 cup medium- or short-grain brown rice, washed and soaked 4 to 6 hours
1⅓ cups filtered water
1-inch strip kombu or pinch sea salt

Drain rice. Place new filtered water, rice, and kombu in stainless steel pot. Bring to a boil over medium-high heat. When boiling, cover with lid, put flame deflector (if you have one) underneath pot and simmer on low flame for 45 minutes.

Turn off flame and fluff rice with a fork or rice paddle.

quinoa with toasted pecans and dried cherries

G 45 • Makes 6 to 8 servings

This recipe is so delicious and great for large groups. It looks more beautiful if you use half regular quinoa and half red quinoa, so give that a try!

1½ cups filtered water, or vegetable broth
1 cup quinoa, rinsed
Pinch sea salt and black pepper
⅓ cup parsley, chopped
1 rib celery, diced
½ cup pecans, toasted
⅓ cup dried cherries, chopped
¼ cup *lemon miso dressing*, on page 89

Bring water or broth to a boil in medium saucepan with quinoa and pinch of sea salt. Simmer, covered, for 20 to 25 minutes, until "tails" fall off the grain. In a large bowl, mix quinoa with other ingredients, including dressing. Allow 15 minutes or more for flavors to meld.

pineapple not-so-fried rice • 161

pineapple not-so-fried rice

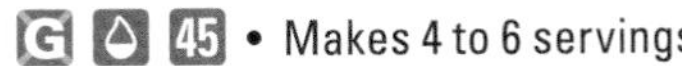 • Makes 4 to 6 servings

I love fried rice, but I don't love all the oil it uses. I came up with this healthier oil-free version that is very similar to the fried rice I used to get at Chinese restaurants growing up. Use as much pineapple as you like, or you can leave it out all together. If you want, you can use brown basmati rice for a heartier dish.

1 cup white basmati rice
Filtered water
1 cup frozen peas, defrosted
1 can (14 ounces) pineapple chunks, juice reserved
1 cup carrot, diced
½ cup asparagus, cut on diagonal
2 tablespoons tamari, to taste
½ cup cilantro leaves, packed (optional)
Toasted sesame seeds, for garnish

Cook rice in filtered water according to package instructions. When rice is done, place in a medium bowl with peas. Meanwhile, bring pineapple juice to a boil and simmer the carrot, asparagus, tamari, and pineapple chunks until veggies are tender but still crunchy, about five minutes. Toss with rice and cilantro, and season, to taste. Garnish with sesame seeds.

---

veggie sushi rolls

G S 45 • Makes 2 to 3 rolls

Sushi is the greatest thing to make with leftover rice. I usually put about one cup of rice per roll, pressed out very thin. Get creative and try different spreads and fillings in your rolls. Just be sure not to put too many fillings inside, because then your roll will be too big to fit in your mouth!

3 cups *pressure cooked brown rice*, on page 153
2 to 3 nori sheets

spread choices

Mustard and/or vegan mayonnaise
Umeboshi paste
Miso
Almond butter
Mock tuna

filling options

Carrot
Celery
Asparagus
Cucumber
Avocado
Tempeh or tofu
Sauerkraut or pickled shiso

Blanch veggies as needed. Fry tempeh/tofu, if using. Lay nori on sushi mat with lines going in a vertical direction. Keep a small bowl of water nearby to wet your fingers. Spread rice along ⅔ of the nori sheet, starting at the bottom and working up. There should be a space at the top with no rice. Wet fingers to help spread the rice evenly.

Lay down your spread, then the fillings, evenly across the bottom, about an inch up from the bottom of the nori. While holding the fillings in place, start to roll the bottom of the nori sheet up over the fillings while tucking them under. Continue to roll and tuck until you reach the end of the nori sheet. If necessary, lightly wet the end to help it stick closed.

blissful tutorial

To see a tutorial on how to make sushi rolls, watch the video on my YouTube channel: www.youtube.com/user/theblissfulchef

"With every drop of water you drink, every breath you take, you're connected to the sea. No matter where on Earth you live."

— Sylvia Earle, American oceanographer

orange-wakame cucumber salad • 172

sea vegetables, huh?

Sea vegetables are an important missing link in the plant-based diet. They are readily available at natural food stores across the country, but that aisle is often neglected. I have to admit that sea vegetables are an acquired taste. When I first starting eating them, I could barely get them down. Now I have found ways to make them more appealing and appetizing. Each one has a different taste, texture, and smell. At the natural food store, you can find dulse, kelp, and nori shakers that make sneaking sea veggies into your diet very easy. Most of the recipes in this section are great for sea-veg newbies.

anytime

sea vegetables

Sea vegetables, or seaweeds, are some of the most nutritious foods we can eat. They have more vitamins and trace minerals per ounce than any other food. They are very alkaline, have antibiotic and antibacterial properties, aid in digestion, and help reduce cholesterol. You don't need to have a lot to get the benefits. Just a tablespoon or two a day will do the trick. Keep in mind that sea vegetables are usually dried and will double or triple in size once rehydrated. Be sure to drain off the soaking water and cook in fresh water. Also, buy your sea vegetables from a reputable source. They may be cheaper at Asian markets, but they also may contain fish by-products or unwanted chemicals.

wakame

Wakame is part of the kelp family. Often found in soups and light salads, it supports the liver and nervous system. Usually it comes in flakes or long strips. If you find it in long strips, use kitchen scissors to cut into ½-inch pieces. For soups, toss in a pinch or two toward the beginning. For salads, marinate the wakame for up to 20 minutes.

kombu

Kombu, also known as kelp, is used mostly while cooking rice, grains, and soups as a flavor enhancer, to help aid in digestion, and to add trace minerals. It's good for the reproductive system, kidneys, and adrenal glands. Generally when cooking grains or beans, add a 1-inch piece of kombu at the beginning of cooking.

nori

Most people recognize nori because of the popularity of sushi. Kids love it for its mild sweet and salty flavor. It has more vitamin A than carrots and is full of calcium, iron, and many trace minerals. It makes the perfect snack, and is beautiful as a garnish for soups, grains, or salads.

dulse

Dulse is one of my favorite sea vegetables. It's a good source of vitamins E, C, and B-complex and strengthens the blood, kidneys, and adrenal glands. It's red in color and does not require cooking. It either comes as whole leaves, in flakes, or in a condiment shaker.

arame/hiziki

Arame is lighter in taste than hiziki. It requires less cooking time and can be marinated for salads. It's a great source of calcium, potassium, and other minerals. It's usually found in long threads, while hiziki is usually found in smaller pellets or thicker strands. I find hiziki to be the strongest-tasting sea vegetable, so it's best when cooked for a longer period of time with other sweeter vegetables. Be sure to soak both of these before using and drain off the soaking liquid.

anytime

dulse-pumpkin seed condiment

G S ⊘ 45 • Makes about ½ cup

This is a very simple macrobiotic condiment that is so tasty and great to serve over grains, salads, or soups. It comes from my friends David and Cynthia Briscoe, who have an online cooking school that can be found in the resources section in the back of the book.

½ pumpkin seeds
½ cup tightly packed dulse (yields about ¼ cup powdered dulse)

Unfold dulse and check for seashells and stones. Spread dulse on a cookie sheet and bake at 350 degrees F for 10 to 15 minutes, or until dulse can be crushed easily. Place pumpkin seeds on another cookie sheet and bake at the same time for 10 to 15 minutes. Stir once after five minutes, so the seeds bake evenly. The seeds are roasted when they puff out and are slightly golden.

Place dulse in a suribachi (see page 21) and grind to a fine powder. Add roasted pumpkin seeds to the powdered dulse and grind with the pestle until about ⅔ of the seeds are crushed.

jeanne's cabbage salad

G S 45 • Makes 5 to 7 servings

This salad comes from my friend Jeanne at the 7th Element Company in Los Angeles. She and her partner have an amazing macrobiotic meal delivery service called Chew. If you live in Southern California, definitely check them out at www.the7thelement.com. If you can't find dulse flakes, then chop up whole dulse finely.

3 cups cabbage, shredded
½ cup cucumbers, cut in thin quarter-moons
¼ cup carrots, shredded
¼ cup radishes, cut in thin quarter-moons
2 tablespoons scallions, chopped thin
3 tablespoons apple cider vinegar
3 tablespoons brown rice vinegar
2 tablespoons olive oil
3 tablespoons dulse flakes

Mix all ingredients together in large bowl. Let sit in the fridge for 15 minutes to let flavors meld, then serve.

fan fave

land and sea soba salad • 169

land and sea soba salad

  • Makes 4 to 6 servings • **FAN FAVE**

This delicious summer salad was inspired by Barb Jurecki-Humphrey's cooking class at the 2009 French Meadows Macro Summer Camp.

Filtered water
1 package (8 ounces) soba noodles (yam or mugwort kinds have more protein)
1 carrot, julienned
3 leaves Napa cabbage, sliced
4 leaves kale, chopped or 1 cup broccoli
1 cup tofu, steamed or fried
Sesame seeds, toasted for garnish
¼ cup hiziki (or arame if not available), soaked in ¾ cup filtered water
2 teaspoons soy sauce or tamari

dressing

⅓ cup soy sauce or tamari
¼ cup brown rice vinegar
2 teaspoons fresh ginger (or just juice)
1 tablespoon liquid smoke
2 tablespoons maple syrup

Cook soba according to directions on package. Whisk dressing ingredients together. Remove noodles from water, toss with dressing, and set aside. Keep water boiling for blanching vegetables. Blanch veggies until lightly cooked and vibrant in color. Remove with skimmer and toss veggies with noodles.

In a small pot, simmer hiziki with new water and soy sauce until all water is absorbed. Steam or fry tofu in a skillet until lightly browned on both sides. Toss all ingredients with noodles and veggies. Sprinkle roasted sesame seeds on top and serve immediately.

mock tuna

• Makes 6 to 8 servings

You will be shocked at how delicious this mock tuna is, without all the saturated fat that comes with the real thing. Walnuts are used in place of salmon for their rich omega-3 content. Sea vegetables like kelp and dulse are used to give a hint of fish flavor while adding nutrient-rich trace minerals to the dish.

1 cup almonds, soaked 4 hours
½ cup walnuts, soaked 4 hours
2 carrots, grated
2 stalks celery, minced
1 lemon, juiced
1 lime, juiced
3 tablespoons kelp granules
2 tablespoons dulse flakes
2 tablespoons nutritional yeast
2 tablespoons dried parsley
1 teaspoon maple syrup or brown rice syrup
1 teaspoon coriander
3 tablespoons tamari
¼ cup filtered water, as needed

Drain nuts, then blend in a food processor until finely ground. Add the rest of the ingredients and blend until almost smooth. Be sure to scrape down the edges of the bowl a few times to incorporate all the ingredients. Serve with crackers or pita bread, as a side dish, or as a filling for *veggie sushi rolls*, on page 161.

soba noodle sushi with apricot-ginger dipping sauce

• Makes 3 sushi rolls • **CHEF FAVE**

This dish is a new take on traditional sushi rolls with noodles instead of rice. It's not only pleasing to the eye and fun to make, it tastes delish. Feel free to use whatever fillings you prefer.

2 bundles from 1 package (19½ ounces) soba noodles
3 collard green leaves, stem removed
3 nori sheets
1 cup purple cabbage, thinly sliced
1 Persian cucumber, thinly sliced
6 basil leaves

apricot-ginger dipping sauce

1 tablespoon apricot preserves
1 teaspoon ginger, minced
2 tablespoons tamari
1 tablespoon maple syrup
1 tablespoon apple cider vinegar
1 tablespoon fresh mint, minced

Cook soba noodles according to package directions. Dip collard greens in the boiling water 15 seconds before you drain the noodles. Drain and shock with cold water.

To assemble the sushi, lay a piece of nori on a sushi mat with the lines going vertically. Lay a collard green leaf on top of the nori, then layer the other veggies and basil toward the bottom of the sheet. Roll up the sushi while tucking the veggies until you roll it all the way up. Be sure to leave some of the nori at the top exposed so you can seal the roll with a little bit of water if needed. Slice into one-inch pieces.

Whisk together the dressing ingredients in a small bowl. Serve with sushi.

soba noodle sushi with apricot-ginger dipping sauce • 170

wakame tofu "bacon" quiche

[icon] • Makes 6 to 8 servings

If you love quiche, you will love this recipe, which has wakame for an added nutritional explosion. It has the perfect quiche-like consistency, so you'll never know it's vegan!

3 slices store-bought tempeh bacon (or use *sizzling tempeh bacon*, on page 45, chopped)
1 package (14 ounces) extra firm tofu, crumbled
3 tablespoons soy sauce or tamari
2 tablespoons tahini
1 tablespoon apple cider or sherry vinegar
1 teaspoon toasted sesame oil
¼ cup nutritional yeast
Spices of your choice: ½ teaspoon each cumin, oregano, basil, paprika, coriander, rosemary, chili powder, black pepper
½ cup red bell pepper, diced
1 medium zucchini, quarter-moons
2 tablespoons dried wakame, soaked for 10 minutes, then drained

If using store-bought tempeh bacon pan-fry, chop, and set aside. Preheat oven to 350 degrees F. Combine tofu, soy sauce, tahini, vinegar, oil, nutritional yeast, and spices in a food processor. Blend until smooth, making sure to scrape the edges of the bowl a few times to incorporate all ingredients.

Place tofu mixture in a medium bowl and combine with the veggies, wakame, and bacon. Place in greased pie pan or 8x8 casserole dish. Bake covered for 40 minutes. Uncover and cook for 15 more minutes, until the top is golden and browned. Serve hot.

blissful variation

To make this a traditional quiche with a crust, use the *homemade flaky crust* recipe, on page 228.

---

orange-wakame cucumber salad

G [icon] 45 • Makes 4 to 6 servings

A light summertime sea vegetable salad, this adds nutrition to any meal. Or serve with rice crackers as a snack.

⅓ cup wakame flakes, soaked three minutes, then drained
2 Persian cucumbers, thinly sliced on the diagonal
1 medium orange, zested and juiced
1 teaspoon maple syrup
2 tablespoons brown rice vinegar
1 tablespoon tamari
1 teaspoon ginger, grated (optional)
Pinch sea salt
1 tablespoon sesame seeds, toasted, for garnish

Combine all ingredients except sesame seeds in a medium bowl and allow to marinate for 15 minutes, stirring occasionally. If it needs more sea salt, season to taste after it marinates. Garnish with sesame seeds and serve.

wakame tofu "bacon" quiche • 172

mustard arame sauté

 • Makes 2 to 3 servings

This dish is savory and satisfying and a great way to sneak in sea vegetables. Be sure to use the stalk of the broccoli; just cut off the woody parts before dicing.

½ cup arame, soaked three minutes, then drained
4 ounces tempeh, cubed
Filtered water
Dash tamari
2 teaspoons sesame oil
1 stalk celery, thinly sliced
1 cup carrots, cut on diagonal
Pinch sea salt
½ cup asparagus, cut on diagonal
1½ cups broccoli, cut into stems and florets and chopped
Dash brown rice vinegar
1 tablespoon stone-ground mustard
Sea salt, to taste

Simmer the arame, tempeh, ⅓ cup water, and tamari in a small saucepan for about five to ten minutes, or until all the liquid is absorbed.

Meanwhile, heat oil in medium skillet over medium flame. Sauté celery and carrots for three minutes, cover with lid, and stir occasionally. Add a pinch of salt, asparagus, and broccoli stems and sauté for two more minutes. Add a splash of water if the veggies begin to stick.

Lastly add the broccoli florets and stir in the arame-tempeh mixture, vinegar, mustard, and a dash of water if necessary. Simmer with lid on for three minutes. Taste and season with tamari if needed.

"I do feel that spiritual progress does demand at some stage that we should cease to kill our fellow creatures for the satisfaction of our bodily wants."

— Mahatma Gandhi

lentil-coconut curry • 184

compassionate proteins

The age-old question posed to all vegans is "Where do you get your protein?" And to this I say, you can find protein in almost all foods. Some have more than others, though, with animal foods being the most concentrated source of protein. But our bodies prefer plant-based proteins, like beans, legumes, grains, nuts, and seeds. These proteins are easier to digest, and do not have the saturated fat and cholesterol that lead to blocked arteries. Since they take less energy to digest, they leave us feeling light and energetic. Many studies suggest that we don't need as much protein as we are led to believe. Everyone's needs are different, but I encourage you to replace some animal-centered proteins with vegetable-quality proteins found in this chapter.

spring

summer

autumn

winter

anytime

plant-based protein basics

Beans are a powerhouse of nutrients, iron, vitamins, and fiber, and free of cholesterol and saturated fat, making them the ideal source of plant-based protein. Below are my favorite beans listed in order of highest protein content along with other protein sources from soy and wheat gluten.

staple beans

Black and yellow soybeans
Green lentils (do not need soaking)
Le Puy (French lentils, do not need soaking)
Azuki
Cannellini (white beans)
Navy
Turtle (black beans)
Anasazi
Split Peas (do not need soaking)
Garbanzo (chickpeas)
Great Northern
Kidney
Lima
Black-eyed peas
Pinto
Mung beans
Fava
Red lentils (do not need soaking)

soy products

Miso
Soy milk, yogurt, cheese
Tempeh
Tofu
Natto

other

Seitan – "wheat meat"

Making your own beans is a snap if you purchase a pressure cooker. Follow the *basic beans* recipe, on page 202, to make pressure-cooked beans. Many people have a hard time digesting beans. If you follow the steps below, you'll be better equipped to make the best-tasting and most digestible beans you've ever had. I prefer to buy organic beans in the bulk bins at my natural food store.

washing and soaking beans

All beans, legumes, and lentils should be washed to remove any dirt and enzyme inhibitors. Sometimes beans from the bulk bins will have stones or other foreign matter mixed in, so be sure to carefully pick through them while you wash. With the exception of lentils and split peas, I like to soak beans to make them more digestible and save time on cooking. I usually do at least a few hours up to overnight in fresh water. Be sure to drain the soaking water and use new water when ready to cook the beans.

cooking beans

Beans can be cooked in two ways, in a pot on the stove or in a pressure cooker. Small beans and lentils can be boiled on the stove while other dried beans can be cooked in a pressure cooker to save time. Place beans in water in a heavy pot or pressure cooker. How much water you use depends on whether you are cooking in a pot or pressure cooker. In a pressure cooker, you need water just to cover the beans. In a pot you need 3½ cups per cup of dried beans. Add a one-inch piece of kombu with the beans to aid in digestion, or put in bay leaves (or both). Kombu also adds many trace minerals and a light flavor to the beans. If using a pressure cooker, follow the manufacturer's instructions. If cooking in a pot, lower the flame and cook until beans are tender (time depends on the bean). With either method, season at the end. Do not put salt in at the beginning.

All canned bean brands at the writing of this book, save for the Eden brand, have BPA in the lining of the aluminum cans, so it's best to avoid canned beans except when in a serious time pinch. BPA stands for Bisphenol A and is a chemical used when making plastic that is harmful to our health. Most of the recipes offer the option of using fresh beans or canned. If you do decide to use canned beans, be sure to drain and wash them thoroughly.

Remember this rule of thumb: ⅔ cup of dried beans = about 1½ cups; cooked = about 1 (15 ounce) can of beans.

tempeh and tofu

There's quite a bit of controversy about soy products these days. You'll even find many soy-free recipes in this cookbook. Personally, I don't think that fermented and traditional soy products (tempeh, tofu, shoyu, tamari, miso, natto) are "bad," but anything in excess is not good. So if you are eating a plant-based diet, choose a variety of protein sources for your meals, not just tofu, and then you don't need to worry, unless you have a serious allergy to soy.

Depending on what brand of tofu you buy, it may be best to press the tofu to get out the excess water before starting a recipe. If the tofu is packed in water, you will get better results with pressing. To press tofu, remove from package, wrap tofu in a clean dish towel and place on cutting board. Put a plate or another cutting board on top of tofu, then place a heavy item on top on that. This could be anything that is about 3 pounds and not so heavy that it smashes the tofu (a large book works well). Leave for 10-15 minutes.

Tempeh and tofu should be steamed or cooked for at least 10 to 15 minutes to aid in digestion. Never eat tempeh and tofu raw. One word of advice–stay away from textured vegetable protein (TVP), analog meat substitutes, and anything that has "soy protein isolates" on the label if possible. TVP is often used in fake meat products. These foods are helpful when you are first transitioning to a plant-based diet, but I wouldn't eat them often. Soy-protein isolate is the stuff people are talking about when they say soy is "bad."

seitan – the other wheat meat

Even more so than soy, many people have developed an allergy to wheat and gluten, because it's in every processed food you can imagine. Seitan is the protein that's left when you remove all the bran and germ from wheat flour and is a great protein source for vegetarians. Its meat-like texture is very versatile, and allows you to create recipes to please both omnivore and herbivore. I don't use it much in this cookbook, but I do in the most delicious *barbecued seitan* recipe, on page 192, you've ever had!

black-eyed pea bbq stew • 182

spring

black-eyed pea bbq stew

 • Makes 4 to 6 servings

This hearty and filling stew will leave you feeling warm and comforted. The black-eyed peas and root vegetables are full of fiber, so it's a great meal to fill you up without much fat or calories.

1 cup dried black-eyed peas, washed
½ cup filtered water
1 cup rutabaga, small cubes
2 celery stalks, diced
1 carrot, diced
Pinch sea salt
½ cup barbecue sauce
1 cup frozen peas
Sea salt and black pepper, to taste

Follow the *basic beans* recipe, on page 202. Meanwhile, in a skillet with lid simmer veggies with a pinch of sea salt and ½ cup water until tender.

When beans are done, drain and return to pressure cooker or pot. Add veggie mixture to beans with barbecue sauce and simmer, covered, for five minutes. Add water as necessary if it starts to stick, and stir occasionally. Stir in peas and season with sea salt and pepper as needed.

blissful variation

To shave off 20 minutes from this recipe feel free to use two 15-ounce cans of black-eyed peas, drained and rinsed, and skip the cooking beans step.

---

blackened tempeh caesar wrap

Makes 4 wraps

Tempeh is one of my favorite plant-based proteins, and it's so good for you. This blackened tempeh is great as a side, in a wrap, or on a sandwich, and will turn anyone into a tempeh lover.

1 package (8 ounces) tempeh
Your favorite brand of tortillas
Lettuce
Carrot, matchsticks
Sprouts
Avocado

blackened tempeh caesar wrap • 182

blackened marinade

¼ cup tamari
2 tablespoons olive oil
2 tablespoons maple syrup
1 tablespoon sherry vinegar
1 tablespoon dried thyme
1 tablespoon paprika
Dash black pepper

Slice tempeh into thin slices. Combine all marinade ingredients inside a glass dish large enough to fit slices of tempeh in one single layer. Coat each piece of tempeh and marinate for one hour, turning once. Drain most of the marinade from the tempeh and save, leaving a little at the bottom of the pan. Bake for 30 to 35 minutes at 375 degrees F, turning once halfway through. If it looks dry at the halfway point, add a touch of the marinade to the pan.

Toast tortillas, then pile on your favorite wrap fillings. Top with the *blissed caesar dressing*, on page 102.

fresh corn and zucchini frittata

G • Makes 5 to 7 servings

When I went vegan, two things I really missed were frittata and quiche. Thankfully, I created this tofu version that is very reminiscent of the egg-based frittatas I used to have. Feel free to change up the vegetables each season for a slightly different flavor.

3 ears corn, cut off the cob
1 medium zucchini, grated
1 package (14 ounces) extra firm tofu
3 tablespoons yellow cornmeal
Pinch sea salt and black pepper
½ teaspoon baking powder
⅓ cup nutritional yeast
1 tablespoon soy sauce or tamari
1 teaspoon maple syrup
2 tablespoons umeboshi vinegar or sherry vinegar

Place veggies in a large bowl. Preheat the oven to 350 degrees F. Combine all remaining ingredients in a food processor. Blend until smooth and no tofu chunks are visible. Be sure to scrape the edges of the bowl a few times to incorporate all the ingredients.

Place tofu mixture in bowl with veggies. Fold in the vegetables until well incorporated. Fill a lightly oiled nine-inch round pie pan with mixture and press evenly into pan, smoothing over the top. Bake for 50 minutes uncovered.

blissful variation

To make this as a quiche, use the *home-made flaky crust* recipe, on page 228.

lentil-coconut curry

G 45 • Makes 4 to 6 servings

This dish is a mix of different flavors and ethnic styles. The curry powder and turmeric give it excellent anti-inflammatory properties.

4 cups filtered water, divided
1 cup green lentils, rinsed
1 tablespoon coconut oil
1 medium carrot, diced
2 celery stalks, diced
Pinch sea salt
1 tablespoon curry powder
1 teaspoon coriander
1 teaspoon turmeric
2 tablespoons tamari
1 tablespoon mirin
1 cup filtered water
1 cup grated unsweetened dried coconut
1 ear fresh corn, cut from cob
Cilantro, for garnish

Bring 3 cups filtered water and lentils to a boil in a medium saucepan. Simmer until almost tender, about 25 minutes. Take care to not overcook the lentils—they will cook in the curry sauce later. Turn off flame and let sit.

Meanwhile, heat large skillet and oil over medium heat. Add carrots, celery, and pinch of sea salt and sauté for a few minutes until lightly cooked. Add spices and sauté for another minute.

Stir in the rest of the ingredients, including lentils. Simmer with lid on for 10 minutes, stirring occasionally. Add water as needed so lentils do not stick. Remove lid and cook for a few more minutes, until water is cooked off. Garnish with cilantro and serve immediately.

blissful variation

Vary this dish by changing out vegetables to whatever is in season and trying different spices to your liking.

---

tempeh reuben with russian dressing

Makes 4 sandwiches

When I first discovered the joys of tempeh reubens at the vegan restaurants around Los Angeles, I would try every one to find the best. My winner was at Café Flourish. It closed down, so I was forced to create my own.

2 packages (8 ounces) tempeh
8 slices rye bread
Earth Balance, for frying bread (optional)
2 avocados, sliced
Lettuce
Sauerkraut

marinade

¼ cup filtered water
¼ cup tamari
¼ cup red wine vinegar
1 teaspoon paprika
½ teaspoon dried dill weed
Dash black pepper
2 tablespoons maple syrup

russian dressing

makes about 1 cup

½ cup vegan mayonnaise
2 tablespoons ketchup
2 tablespoons relish, or chopped pickles
½ tablespoon red wine vinegar
½ tablespoon tamari, or more to taste

curry chicken-less salad • 187

Cut the thickness of the tempeh in half, then cut into 3x2 cutlets. Mix marinade ingredients in a long, shallow dish. Marinate tempeh for three hours or overnight, flipping a few times. Preheat oven to 350 degrees F. Drain most of the marinade from the tempeh and save, leaving a little at the bottom of the pan. Bake for 40 minutes, flipping tempeh at 20 minutes. If it gets too dry, add a touch of marinade.

Meanwhile, whisk together the dressing ingredients until smooth and creamy.

to assemble the reuben

Heat cast-iron skillet over medium flame. Spread Earth Balance on one side of each slice of bread. Fry butter-side-down first until golden brown and crispy. Flip and fry the other side. Continue with the rest of the bread.

Cut tempeh into slices to fit bread and place a few slices on one piece of bread. Top with avocado. Place desired amount of sauerkraut on top of avocado, then smother in *russian dressing*, on page 185, and top with lettuce. Top with another slice of bread and cut in half. Serve immediately.

blissful suggestion

Great served with *root fries*, on page 120, or *chilled corn bisque* on page 66.

summer

curry chicken-less salad

45 • Makes 5 to 7 servings • **FAN FAVE**

This is the perfect lunch and is delicious whether it has the curry powder or not. If you aren't feeling like curry, leave it out.

1 package (14 ounces) extra firm tofu
4 ounces tempeh (optional)
¼ cup carrot, grated
1 cup celery, finely diced
¼ cup currants
¼ cup slivered almonds
1 tablespoon curry powder, or more to taste
½ cup vegan mayonnaise
1 tablespoon yellow mustard
1 teaspoon maple syrup
1 tablespoon apple cider vinegar
Sea salt and black pepper, to taste
Whole-wheat bread, pita, or brown rice crackers

Steam tofu and tempeh for 10 minutes. Allow it to cool enough to handle, then grate into medium bowl and stir in the rest of the salad ingredients. Mix until well combined. Season to taste.

Chill in refrigerator for 15 to 30 minutes. Serve on toasted bread or with brown rice crackers.

blissful suggestion

Experiment with different dried or fresh herbs for this salad.

---

hawaiian tofu and veggie kabobs

G 45 • Makes 3 to 5 servings

This is a big hit with the kids, as one of my recipe testers found out. Her son kept asking for more tofu! Feel free to try your favorite veggies with this marinade. Tempeh is a delicious alternative to tofu.

Oil, for grill
1 package (14 ounces) extra firm tofu, cut into 2-inch cubes
1 red bell pepper, seeded and cut into large chunks
1 zucchini, sliced into 1-inch pieces
6 to 8 cremini mushrooms, ends trimmed
6 large cherry tomatoes
Pineapple chunks, fresh or canned

hawaiian bbq marinade

1 cup barbecue sauce
¼ cup maple syrup
2 tablespoons apple cider vinegar
1 tablespoon Dijon mustard
1 cup pineapple juice
Pinch sea salt and black pepper

Mix marinade in long, shallow dish. Marinate tofu and veggies for at least one hour, up to overnight, stirring occasionally. If grilling, skewers should be soaked in filtered water for 20 minutes to prevent burning. Also, make sure your grill is properly oiled so the tofu doesn't stick.

Alternate tofu and veggies with pineapple on the skewers. Continue until all the ingredients are used. Cook on grill until all sides are brown, basting with leftover marinade.

> **blissful suggestion**
>
> You can use the *homemade bbq sauce*, on page 193, or store-bought barbecue sauce for this recipe.

---

laotian tofu larb

 • Makes 4 to 6 servings

Larb is a traditional Thai and Laotian dish usually made with chicken or pork, lime juice, spices, and peanuts. This is a healthy, delicious plant-based version made with tofu and lots of added veggies.

1 package (14 ounces) extra firm tofu
1 large carrot, grated
5 leaves Napa cabbage, thinly sliced
1 cup red bell pepper, finely diced
¼ cup cilantro, chopped
3 tablespoons mint, finely chopped
1 lime, juiced
3 tablespoons tamari
2 tablespoons maple syrup
Pinch sea salt
⅓ cup unsalted roasted peanuts, for garnish

Steam tofu for 10 minutes. Crumble tofu into a bowl. Add all ingredients except peanuts to the bowl and stir well. Chill for 15 to 30 minutes to let flavors meld. Garnish with peanuts.

---

tofu salad (eggless egg salad)

45 • Makes 3 to 5 servings

People go crazy for egg salad. It's always on the salad bar and available at every deli. Personally, I never got into it until I made this vegan version. It's so reminiscent of the real thing—but without the heart attack.

1 package (14 ounces) extra firm tofu
2 celery stalks, small dice
1 medium carrot, grated (optional)
¼ cup vegan mayonnaise
1 tablespoon relish or 2 tablespoons chopped dill pickles
1 tablespoon Dijon or yellow mustard
1 tablespoon soy sauce or tamari
1 teaspoon turmeric
1 teaspoon celery salt
Dash black pepper

Steam tofu for 10 minutes. Cool. Using your hands, crumble tofu into a medium bowl. Add the rest of the ingredients and mix gently but thoroughly. Serve as a sandwich filling or on a bed of greens.

tropical three-bean salad • 189

tropical three-bean salad

   45 • Makes 5 to 7 servings

This salad is made with three of my favorite types of beans, which I like to cook from scratch. They can all be soaked in the same bowl and cooked together in a pot or pressure cooker because they take about the same time to cook.

½ cup dried kidney beans, soaked 5 to 8 hours, or 1 can (15 ounces), drained and rinsed
½ cup dried white beans, soaked 5 to 8 hours, or 1 can (15 ounces), drained and rinsed
½ cup dried chickpeas, soaked 5 to 8 hours, or 1 can (15 ounces), drained and rinsed
1-inch piece kombu
1 mango, chopped
Pinch sea salt and black pepper
1 large heirloom tomato, chopped (or 2 cups Roma tomato)
1 avocado, cubed
1 lime, juiced
1 teaspoon cumin
Dash cinnamon and coriander
Sea salt, to taste

If you have a pressure cooker, cook all three beans together according to manufacturer's directions with a piece of kombu, then drain, discard kombu, and place in medium bowl.

Let beans cool slightly, then combine all ingredients with beans and allow 15 minutes for flavors to meld. Add sea salt, as needed.

baked oil-free falafel with tzatziki sauce • 191

autumn

baked oil-free falafel with tzatziki sauce

• Makes 12 patties

I love falafel, but most recipes and the store-bought kind are full of oil. So I created this oil-free version that is baked instead of fried. Of course, you can fry these if that is what you prefer. This is a great way to use leftover chickpeas. Serve with tzatziki sauce (recipe follows) in a pita, in a wrap, or on their own.

Oil, for pan
1 cup dried chickpeas, washed and soaked 6 to 8 hours
2 tablespoons tamari
⅓ cup cilantro leaves, packed
⅓ cup flat-leaf parsley leaves, packed
1 teaspoon coriander
1 teaspoon cumin
2 tablespoons flax meal
Dash black pepper
Dash paprika
¼ cup breadcrumbs, plus some for pan

Follow the *basic beans* recipe on page 202 for cooking chickpeas. Then preheat oven to 350 degrees F. Drain chickpeas and put them in a food processor with all the ingredients except the breadcrumbs. Blend until well combined, making sure to scrape down the edges of the bowl a few times to incorporate all the ingredients. Add the breadcrumbs and blend for one more minute.

Lightly oil a muffin pan. Then sprinkle breadcrumbs in each tin to barely coat the bottom. Put about 2 tablespoons of the falafel mixture in each tin and lightly press down. Bake for 20 minutes, then flip each patty, lightly press back down, and bake another 20 minutes.

---

tzatziki sauce

Makes about 1 cup

This is a healthy vegan version of the popular Mediterranean tzatziki sauce traditionally served with meals. It would also be great in a wrap, on a baked potato, or used in place of tartar sauce.

1 package Mori Nu silken tofu
2 tablespoons lemon juice
1 tablespoon dill weed
1 tablespoon tamari
Dash black pepper
Dash paprika
1 teaspoon maple syrup

barbecued seitan • 192

1 tablespoon nutritional yeast
2 tablespoons fresh parsley
⅓ cup pickles, finely chopped

Blend all the ingredients except pickles until smooth. Fold in pickles. Chill for 10 minutes before serving.

---

barbecued seitan

Makes 3 to 4 servings

This seitan is very meat-like and is great cut into "cutlet" pieces with BBQ sauce drizzled on top or chopped finely for a pulled-pork-like texture served on a whole-wheat bun.

Oil, for steamer basket and cookie sheet
1 cup vital wheat gluten
2 tablespoons nutritional yeast
½ teaspoon paprika
½ teaspoon coriander
Dash black pepper
½ cup *homemade bbq sauce* (recipe follows) or store-bought
⅓ cup vegetable broth
1 tablespoon tamari
1 tablespoon balsamic vinegar
2 tablespoons cashew butter
1 teaspoon liquid smoke

Mix first five dry ingredients in a medium bowl. In a small bowl, whisk together all the wet ingredients except oil. Pour the wet ingredients into the dry ingredients and mix thoroughly. Knead the dough into a ball for about five minutes, then let dough rest for 20 minutes.

Meanwhile, place steamer basket in a medium pot with an inch of water. Spray basket lightly with oil. Cut seitan into two pieces and place on steamer basket. Cover, bring to a boil, then steam for 10 minutes. Preheat oven to 350 degrees F.

Take each piece of seitan and cut into 3x2 "cutlet" pieces. Spray cookie sheet lightly with oil and place seitan pieces on the sheet. Bake for 15 minutes, flip, and bake another 10 minutes.

---

homemade bbq sauce

G 🔥 45 • Makes about 5 cups

Sure, it's quicker to just buy a bottle of barbeque sauce, but making it from scratch is super easy and delicious! If you can't find barley malt, you can substitute molasses.

1 can (28 ounces) tomato puree or sauce
⅓ cup filtered water, or less, to desired thickness
2 tablespoons apple cider vinegar
2 tablespoons balsamic vinegar
1 tablespoon Dijon mustard, dissolved in vinegars
1 tablespoon tamari
¼ cup maple syrup
¼ cup barley malt
1 tablespoon vegan Worcester sauce
1 tablespoon chili powder
Pinch sea salt and black pepper

Whisk together all ingredients in a medium saucepan over medium heat until combined. Simmer 10 to 15 minutes. Refrigerate up to one week.

blissful two-bean harvest chili

G S 🔥 45 • Makes 6 to 8 servings

Personally, I like my chili with lots of vegetables. It ups the nutritional value and taste of the dish. So this isn't your usual chili recipe. If you want, you can leave out the veggies, but definitely try it at least once as is. This recipe makes a ton, so it's great to freeze for later use.

1 cup dried pinto beans, soaked 6 to 8 hours, or 1 can (15 ounces), drained and rinsed
2 cups dried black beans, soaked 6 to 8 hours, or 2 cans (15 ounces each), drained and rinsed
1 cup filtered water
2 cups kabocha squash, ½ inch cube, skin on
Pinch sea salt
1 cup celery, diced
1 cup bell pepper, large dice
1 cup fresh corn, off the cob
1 clove garlic, chopped (optional)
2 tablespoons cumin
1 tablespoon oregano
2 tablespoons chili powder
Dash cinnamon
Dash black pepper
1 cup tomatoes, diced
1 can (15 ounces) tomato sauce
Sea salt, to taste
Cilantro, for garnish

Follow the *basic beans* recipe on page 202 for cooking beans from scratch. Save cooking liquid. Meanwhile, heat 1 cup water in a medium skillet over medium flame. Cook kabocha with a pinch of sea salt, covered, until almost tender. Add the rest of the veggies, spices, tomatoes, and sauce. Bring to a boil and then simmer, covered, for five minutes. Stir in beans, with some of the cooking liquid if needed, depending on how chunky you want your chili. Season to taste and simmer another five minutes. Serve hot, garnished with cilantro.

---

tempeh "fish" tacos

  • Makes 3 to 4 servings

If you miss the taste of fish but don't want the added mercury in your diet, try this healthier tempeh version. The tempeh "fish" pieces can be either baked or fried. The fried version will be more reminiscent of fish, but the baked version is oil-free and healthier. Best served with mango-peach salsa *(recipe follows).*

Oil, for pan
1 package (8 ounces) tempeh
1¾ cups unsweetened rice milk
1 tablespoon Dijon mustard
1 tablespoon soy sauce or tamari
½ teaspoon paprika
2 tablespoons dulse flakes
1 tablespoon nutritional yeast
¼ cup cornmeal
½ cup panko-style breadcrumbs
1 tablespoon arrowroot
Corn tortillas, for tacos
1 avocado, sliced

Preheat oven to 350 degrees F. Spray a baking sheet with oil. Cut tempeh into 2-inch long and ½-inch thick pieces. Whisk together wet ingredients and set aside. Place dry ingredients in a food processor and pulse a few times, until the mixture is a fine flour. Place in a small bowl. Dredge each piece of tempeh in the rice milk mixture, then toss with breadcrumb mix. Place on baking sheet in three rows about an inch apart. Spray oil on top of pieces, then bake for 15 minutes. Flip and bake another 15 minutes. Serve immediately in corn tortilla with sliced avocado and *mango-peach salsa*.

blissful variation

To fry tempeh "fish," heat a medium skillet over medium-high flame with about ¼ an inch of safflower oil. When oil is hot, gently place battered tempeh pieces in oil and fry on each side until golden brown. Drain on a paper towel.

---

mango-peach salsa

   • Makes about 2 cups

This salsa is the perfect summertime treat. Serve with chips as an appetizer, in a wrap, or with the tempeh "fish" tacos.

½ cup red bell pepper, minced
1 cup white peach, small cube
1 cup mango, small chunks
½ cup cilantro leaves
½ teaspoon cumin
¼ teaspoon sea salt
Dash black pepper
Dash paprika
Dash cayenne

Combine all ingredients in a medium bowl. Let sit in the fridge for 15 minutes to let the flavors meld.

maple-glazed tempeh • 195

maple-glazed tempeh

 • Makes 3 to 4 servings

You know you wanted one more tempeh recipe! The sweet orange marinade makes this a dish that everyone will love. It can be served with a grain and steamed greens for a macrobiotic meal, or cut the tempeh into cubes and toss with soba noodles and steamed veggies.

1 package (8 ounces) tempeh, cut into cutlets

orange marinade

1 orange, zested and juiced
¼ cup barley malt or maple syrup
1 tablespoon tamari
1 tablespoon brown rice or sherry vinegar
1 tablespoon mirin
1 teaspoon ground coriander
Pinch sea salt and black pepper

Whisk together marinade ingredients and put into an 8x8 baking dish. Marinate tempeh for one hour or more, turning occasionally. Bake at 300 degrees F for 25 minutes, flipping once at the halfway point.

blissful variation

If you want to make the tempeh more savory, reduce the barley malt and add spices that are more savory like cumin, chili powder, or curry.

winter

azuki beans with squash and chestnuts

 • Makes 4 to 6 servings

This is a very traditional macrobiotic dish and it happens to be one of my all-time favorites, so I wanted to include it in this book. Azuki beans and winter squash are a match made in heaven. Feel free to leave out the chestnuts if they're not readily available.

1 cup dried azuki beans, washed, and soaked 6 to 8 hours
½ cup dried chestnuts, soaked 6 to 8 hours
2 cups winter squash, like kabocha, seeded and cubed
1-inch piece kombu
Filtered water
Tamari, to taste

Drain beans and chestnuts. Place in pressure cooker with squash, kombu, and water, filling just until beans are covered. Bring to pressure over medium flame. When full pressure is reached, simmer for 12 minutes. Let the pressure come down naturally. Open lid and stir in tamari. Replace lid and leave for five minutes.

macro mole enchiladas

Makes 4 to 6 servings

These are as close to macrobiotic as mole enchiladas can be. I left out chili powder to make it macro, but feel free to add some if you aren't avoiding nightshades. The Daiya vegan cheese sprinkled on top is optional if you are not eating processed foods or you're watching your weight, but it's pretty heavenly with the cheese!

filling

1 cup of dried white navy beans, soaked 4 to 6 hours
1 tablespoon oil
1 garnet yam, small cubes
Pinch sea salt
1 teaspoon cumin
2 medium zucchini, matchsticks
1 package (10 ounces) mushrooms, sliced
12 corn tortillas
Daiya cheese (optional)

mole sauce

makes about 3½ cups

3 cups vegetable broth
½ cup pumpkin seeds, washed
½ cup pecans, washed
5 tablespoons cocoa powder
3 teaspoons arrowroot
1 cup raisins

1 teaspoon maple syrup
1 teaspoon oregano
2 teaspoons cumin
2 teaspoons coriander
2 dashes cinnamon
2 dashes nutmeg
Pinch sea salt and black pepper

Combine all *mole sauce* ingredients in a blender and blend until well combined and creamy. If using dried beans follow the *basic beans* recipe, on page 202.

While beans are cooking, heat skillet with oil and sauté yam with a pinch of salt until just tender. Add cumin and zucchini and sauté for another five minutes. Cover with lid while sautéing and add a touch of water if the veggies start to stick. Add mushrooms and sauté for another three minutes. Strain cooked beans and stir into veggie mix.

Preheat oven to 350 degrees F. Steam tortillas lightly. Place a small amount of filling and wrap tortilla like an enchilada. Place in a lightly oiled casserole dish and continue with the rest of the filling and tortillas, laying them side by side. Pour *mole sauce* over the top, coating well. Sprinkle Daiya cheese on top if using and bake for 20 minutes. Serve immediately.

pan-fried tofu with carrot-ginger sauce

G • Makes 3 to 5 servings

This recipe is bursting with flavor and health benefits. Ginger adds zest and flavor to a carrot sauce full of beta-carotene and antioxidants. It's a tasty protein dish that doesn't pack on the pounds. My recipe tester's son tried this and it was the only way he ever loved tofu!

1 package (14 ounces) extra firm tofu
1 tablespoon sesame oil, for frying
Cilantro, for garnish

marinade

½ cup orange juice (fresh or bottled)
1 tablespoon soy sauce or tamari
3 tablespoons cilantro, chopped
1 garlic clove, minced (optional)
1 teaspoon ginger, grated

carrot-ginger sauce

2 medium carrots, chopped
2 teaspoons ginger, grated
½ cup orange juice
Leftover marinade

Drain tofu, cut lengthwise in fours, then cut each piece in half. Place in a single layer in a pan that will allow the marinade to cover tofu. Whisk together juice, soy sauce, cilantro, garlic, and ginger, then pour over tofu. Cover and refrigerate overnight, turning once.

Drain the tofu and save the marinade for the sauce. Heat sesame oil in a cast-iron skillet and fry tofu until golden brown on both sides. Add a touch of water if it begins to stick. Remove and drain on paper towel.

Put carrots and sauce ingredients in a saucepan, bring to a boil, then reduce heat and simmer until carrots are soft, about seven minutes. Allow to cool slightly, then add to food processor with leftover marinade. Blend until smooth and no large chunks remain.

To serve, layer pan-fried tofu with carrot sauce on top. Garnish with cilantro.

---

millet-black bean burgers

Makes 12 to 15 burgers

These burgers may take some time and hard work, but they are definitely worth it. They can easily be frozen in a re-sealable plastic bag, so you'll never be out of healthy burgers.

Oil spray, for pan and dish
1 cup dried black beans, washed and soaked 6 hours, or 2 cans (15 ounces each), drained and rinsed
1 cup millet, washed and drained (can be leftover grain or made the day before)
2⅓ cups filtered water
Pinch sea salt
1 tablespoon safflower oil (plus more if frying burger patty)
1 medium sweet potato, small dice/cubes
2 celery stalks, diced
1 teaspoon cumin
1 teaspoon chili powder
1 teaspoon oregano
½ cup sunflower seeds, pan-roasted
1 cup rolled oats
½ cup cornmeal
¼ cup nutritional yeast
3 tablespoons flax meal
1 tablespoon arrowroot

pan-fried tofu with carrot-ginger sauce • 198

¼ cup tamari
Dash black pepper
Cayenne, if you want to make it spicy

If using dried beans, follow the *basic beans* recipe, on page 202. When done, drain beans but save the cooking liquid, in case the burger mixture is dry. Cool beans.

To cook millet, roast in a medium saucepan until dry and fragrant, stirring continuously for about 10 minutes. Slowly add in water and pinch of salt. Bring to boil over medium flame, then cover and simmer on low for 25 minutes. Remove lid and let sit until cool enough to handle (or place in bowl to cool faster).

While your millet is cooking, heat oil in skillet over medium flame. Sauté sweet potato with a pinch of salt for a few minutes, with pan covered, stirring occasionally. Add celery and spices and sauté for a few minutes more. If the veggies begin to stick, you can add a bit of water to the pan. In a separate skillet, dry-roast the sunflower seeds over medium flame until golden.

Preheat oven to 375 degrees F. Combine the millet-vegetable mixture with the rest of the dry ingredients in a big bowl. I like to mash it all together with my hands to make sure the ingredients are incorporated. Fold in beans and sunflower seeds until well combined. If the mixture seems dry and not holding together in your palm, add some of the bean cooking liquid.

Lightly spray a 9x13 glass dish with oil. Press mixture evenly into dish and bake for 35 minutes. Remove and let cool slightly. Cut into squares. If freezing, cut squares out of parchment paper to layer between each burger. Store in a re-sealable plastic bag or glass container with lid.

To serve, it's best to pan-fry in a bit of oil on both sides until brown and crispy. I press them down with a spatula as I do this to make a thinner patty.

blissful suggestion

The patties can be eaten alone as a side dish or on a toasted bun with your favorite burger toppings.

blissful variation

To make into burger shape, form the mixture with your hands or use a 3-inch cookie cutter lightly oiled and place the patties on a parchment–lined cookie sheet to bake.

---

tofu with almond-coconut cilantro sauce

G 45 • Makes 4 to 6 servings

Tofu is very versatile because it takes on whatever flavor you pair it with. This sauce is rich and creamy, yet full of protein. This dish is great served with steamed greens and brown rice.

1 tablespoon coconut oil, for skillet
1 package (14 ounces) extra firm tofu, cut in half, then in ½-inch-thick slices

almond-coconut cilantro sauce

⅓ cup creamy unsalted almond butter
1 can (13½ ounces) unsweetened coconut milk
1 tablespoon fresh ginger, grated
1 tablespoon lime juice

1 tablespoon mirin
1 tablespoon brown rice or maple syrup
1 tablespoon tamari
Pinch sea salt and black pepper
1 bunch cilantro, ½ cup for sauce, some for garnish

Heat oil in skillet over medium-high flame. Lightly fry tofu on both sides until golden brown. Set aside on paper towel. Blend all sauce ingredients in blender or food processor until smooth. Return tofu to skillet. Stir in sauce and simmer until slightly reduced. Garnish with cilantro.

anytime

basic beans

 • Makes 3 to 5 servings

This is the way to make the best, most digestible, awesomely fresh beans you've ever had. This technique is for cooking beans in a pressure cooker and can be used with any of the heartier beans that need to be soaked. Once you make your beans from scratch, you'll never go back. See page 178 for which beans do not need to be soaked.

1 cup dried beans, soaked 6 to 8 hours
1-inch piece kombu
Filtered water to cover beans
Spices of your choice
Pinch sea salt or tamari

Combine beans and water in the pressure cooker, then cover. Heat over medium-high flame. Skim off any foam that forms when beans begin to boil. This is a trick to reduce gas and bloating. Add the kombu to the pot. Wet the gasket of the lid and lock it in place. Follow the manufacturer's instructions regarding cooking times for different beans.

When beans are done, turn off flame and let the pressure come down. Or, if you are in a hurry, you can run cold water over the cooker inside the sink. Stand back if you do this. Unlock lid and remove kombu. Either drain the liquid, then season and add spices, or, if you want the beans more creamy, keep some of the water, season, and continue to cook over low flame in the cooker for a few minutes.

blissful suggestion

If you are using *basic beans* in another recipe they probably don't need any spices added to them. If you plan on having beans as a side dish you can season them depending on what kind of flavor you want or if your meal is of a certain ethnicity. Experiment with different spices and different kinds of beans.

---

indian pizza with mango chutney

G • Makes 7 to 9 servings

I love making pizza crust with polenta. It's a healthier, gluten-free alternative that you can use anytime. I was craving something unique

basic beans • 202

instead of your standard tomato sauce with veggies and cheese, so I came up with this Indian pizza. And what better sauce than a homemade mango chutney.

Oil spray, for dish

for the pizza

1 recipe *basic polenta*, on page 144
½ cup filtered water
2 cups cauliflower florets
1 cup red bell pepper, thinly sliced in 2-inch strips
2 cups mushrooms, thinly sliced
1 teaspoon curry powder
1 teaspoon garam masala
1 cup cooked chickpeas, or 1 can (15 ounces), drained and rinsed
1 tablespoon tamari

mango chutney

makes about 1½ cups

½ cup coconut palm sugar
¼ cup red wine vinegar
Pinch sea salt
2 cups frozen mango, defrosted, chopped finely
¼ cup golden raisins
1 tablespoon ginger, grated
Dash red pepper flakes
Dash coriander
¼ teaspoon curry powder

For the chutney, combine sugar and vinegar in a small saucepan and bring to a boil over medium-high heat. Reduce flame to low and simmer for five minutes. Add the rest of the ingredients and bring back to a boil. Simmer, uncovered for 45 minutes, stirring occasionally. Meanwhile, make your polenta pizza crust and toppings.

Make polenta, pouring the cooked mixture into a 9x13 casserole dish. Let cool completely so that the polenta is pulling from the sides, about one hour. Spray a baking sheet lightly with oil and when set, carefully flip the polenta out into the baking sheet, trying not to break the polenta. Bake at 350 degrees F for 30 minutes. Meanwhile, water sauté veggies with spices, chickpeas, and tamari with the lid on. Stir occasionally and cook over medium flame until the cauliflower is tender, about 10 minutes. Remove lid and cook until all the water is absorbed.

To assemble the pizza, spread the chutney all over the polenta pizza crust, then top with veggie mixture. Bake pizza at 350 degrees F for 15 minutes. Cut into squares; use a spatula to remove pizza from baking sheet.

---

tofu feta cheeze

G • Makes about 2 cups

I learned how to make this pseudo feta cheese in culinary school. You'll be amazed how much this tastes like the real thing. Perfect for salads, to add to pasta, or spread on a sandwich.

¼ cup sweet white miso
¼ cup umeboshi vinegar
2 tablespoons dried basil
2 tablespoons dried oregano
1 teaspoon black peppercorns
1 package (14 ounces) extra firm tofu
Cold-pressed extra virgin olive oil

Mix miso, vinegar, and herbs in a small bowl. Crumble tofu into small-medium pieces into the bowl and mix thoroughly. Place mixture inside an airtight jar and press it down inside (a Mason jar is great). Pour in olive oil until it covers the tofu completely. Cure in refrigerator for at least two days, or up to two weeks. When you want to use the feta, take what you need from the jar with a clean spoon and squeeze out excess oil if needed.

indian pizza with mango chutney • 202

un-tuna salad

G 45 • Makes 3 to 5 servings • **CHEF FAVE**

You would not believe how much this tastes like the tuna fish salad your mom used to make. If you have the time to cook the chickpeas from scratch you won't regret it.

1 cup dried chickpeas, soaked 6 to 8 hours, or 2 cans (15 ounces each), drained and rinsed
1 cup celery, diced
1 medium carrot, grated
¼ cup vegan mayonnaise
2 tablespoons relish, or dill pickle, chopped fine
1 tablespoon yellow mustard
1 tablespoon tamari
1 tablespoon kelp granules (optional)
Season to taste

If using dried beans, follow the *basic beans* recipe, on page 202. Drain beans and place in medium bowl. Mash chickpeas and combine with the rest of ingredients until well mixed. Add sea salt as necessary. Serve with rice crackers, as a sandwich, or wrapped in a tortilla.

blissful variation

Add a tablespoon of curry powder to liven it up.

"Happiness is life served up with a scoop of acceptance, a topping of tolerance and sprinkles of hope, although chocolate sprinkles also work."

— Robert Brault

orange-kissed almond macaroons with chocolate ganache topping • 234

healthier desserts you crave

Everyone loves desserts! These recipes use sweeteners like brown rice syrup, barley malt, maple syrup, and coconut palm sugar, so you can have your dessert, but not have your insulin go on a rollercoaster ride. These foods not only taste good, but they keep you healthy, too. You will also find many gluten-free, oil-free, and wheat-free desserts.

spring

summer

autumn

winter

anytime

blissful tips for baking/dessert making

- Get everything you need together (*mise en place*), then preheat your oven right before you start mixing. Never let your mixed batter/dough sit unless the recipe calls for it.

- My flours of choice for baking are whole-wheat pastry flour, barley, spelt, oat, kamut, brown rice, quinoa, almond, and garbanzo/fava. I rarely use unbleached white flour or whole-wheat and never use bleached white flour. That's just my preference. I encourage you to play around with different flours. Most often, I mix two different kinds. Also, remember that the type of flour you use and the amount of time it's been sitting in your pantry will determine the amount of liquid needed in the recipe. If you are making something that seems to be too liquidy, you can add more flour to round it out.

- Mix your dry ingredients together in a bigger bowl, wet ingredients in a smaller bowl. You don't necessarily need to sift your dry ingredients, I use a whisk to combine everything well. Pour wet ingredients into dry ingredients and fold them together.

- You'll need to have aluminum-free baking powder and baking soda just for baking (that's not used to absorb odor in the fridge). Most desserts need at least a pinch of good-quality sea salt.

- When using liquid sweeteners, rub a bit of olive oil inside your measuring cups and spoons for easy, quick removal of the sweetener.

- Desserts are better with a little fat. I use oils instead of margarine. My favorites for baking are safflower, coconut, olive, avocado, and grapeseed. Canola is a poor-quality oil, so try to shy away from it. Coconut oil is solid at room temperature, so always melt it down before using. Often I use nut butters instead of oil. If you are trying to go sans oil, applesauce or prune puree are good alternatives.

- For egg substitutes, I tend to stick with more whole foods, like flax meal mixed with water or applesauce, mashed bananas, or arrowroot mixed with water or juice. I never use cornstarch because it's poor-quality, highly processed, and often GMO. If possible, replace it with its healthier counterparts, arrowroot or kudzu, if possible. Arrowroot is a white powder used as a thickening agent, just like cornstarch and kudzu. Kudzu comes from the kudzu plant grown in Japan and is good for strengthening the digestive tract. It's more medicinal but also more expensive, so feel free to use arrowroot. You can use egg replacer too, but I rarely do. When using these powders, be sure to dilute them in cold or room temperature liquid first, or they

will clump up when added to the mixture being cooked.

- Liquid and granulated sweeteners cannot be substituted for each other. Baking is a science, and making this switch would throw everything off in the recipe. If a recipe calls for one kind of granulated sugar, however, you can substitute a different granulated sugar. The taste may be slightly different, but it should give the same texture. If you can't locate one of the natural sweeteners below, you are welcome to use sucanut, turbinado, cane sugar, or organic vegan sugar. They wouldn't be my first choice, because they are more refined, but use the highest-quality sweetener available to you.

- I use vanilla flavoring because it does not contain alcohol and I prefer the taste to vanilla extract. Other flavors of extracts will have alcohol; it's hard to avoid.

- For dairy substitutes, I prefer unsweetened rice milk or almond milk, but soy milk is fine, too. Mixing apple cider vinegar with nondairy milk helps baked goods rise and be soft and crumbly. If a recipe calls for any dairy substitute, try to find an unsweetened version to avoid the refined sugar, but don't sweat it if all you can find is sweetened.

- Agar-agar, which is a sea vegetable that has a texture similar to gelatin, is used in a few recipes in the flake form. It's important that all the flakes dissolve when boiling down the agar-agar. Don't be tempted to take a shortcut, because you will have little chewy gelatin chunks in your dessert. If you choose to use agar-agar powder, you need a lot less and it takes less time to dissolve. Once the agar-agar has dissolved and is allowed to cool, it will set like gelatin.

- Nuts are always interchangeable and optional. If you prefer one nut over another, go for it. Just make sure to use raw nuts for baking. If you want to leave them out, that's fine too.

- Silken tofu is often used to make creamy desserts and sauces. The best brands are Mori Nu and Nasoya, and I prefer the organic one. Firmness doesn't matter with silken tofu. If a recipe calls for regular tofu, use extra firm, not the silken variety.

natural sweeteners

There should be no reason why you can't enjoy a healthy sweet every once in a while. Some sweeteners are better than others, though. If you are going to indulge in a dessert, try to use one of the unrefined sweeteners below to keep from having an insulin spike, or "sugar crash," causing an extreme high followed by an extreme low. All of these can be found at your local natural food store or online. They are listed in alphabetical order, not by how often I use them. You'll find the ones I like most are used throughout this book.

agave nectar

Agave is made from the juice of the agave cactus. It's been under scrutiny because of its refining process. It is sweeter than refined sugar, but it is low on the glycemic index and does not increase insulin secretion. I think if you use it moderately, like a touch in your tea sometimes, that is fine. But I don't use it as my regular sweetener.

amasake

Amasake is a fermented drink made from sweet rice. It has a very thick, creamy texture, like a smoothie, and usually comes in small cartons from a company called Amazake. It's great straight if you want a healthy dessert, and it also makes a great base for sauces, custards, and puddings.

barley malt

This is made when barley is fermented, turning the grain into sugar. It is thick, dark, and sticky like brown rice syrup but isn't as sweet as the other natural sweeteners. It's perfect to use in place of molasses in recipes.

brown rice syrup

This is a sweetener that is made when brown rice is ground, cooked, and mixed with enzymes that change it into maltose. Since it's made from a complex carbohydrate, it gives you a slower release of insulin. It has a thick, sticky texture and is less sweet than maple syrup. In recipes, it's interchangeable with other liquid sweeteners, but I often do half brown rice syrup and half maple syrup for a bit more sweetness.

coconut nectar and palm sugar

These sweeteners are the new kids on the block and are some of my favorites. Palm sugar makes the perfect granulated substitute for regular sugar, and it has a low glycemic index. The nectar has a similar texture to brown rice syrup, and the taste is a cross between agave and brown rice syrup.

dates and date sugar

Dates are a great natural sweetener to use, since the fruit is packed with fiber, nutrients, and minerals, which you get whether you use the date or date sugar. Date sugar is the granulated form and can be used to directly replace sugar in recipes (though it won't be as sweet). Date sugar is best used in baking, while the actual dates can be soaked and pureed for any recipe. The perfect no-bake crust is made by processing dates with raw nuts (see *springtime lemon bars*, on page 214).

fruit

Fruits are naturally sweet, with many beneficial vitamins and minerals, so it's the ideal choice if you are craving something sweet. Fruit won't necessarily be enough sweetness for baked goods, but will make a nice addition in terms of texture and flavor. You'll find a few desserts in here that are essentially fruit dressed up, and those are great if you are trying to reduce the amount of sugar and baked goods in your diet.

maple syrup and maple granules

Maple syrup is a sweetener made by boiling the sap of maple trees. The liquid and the granules can be used in baking. You can substitute equally maple granules for sugar or maple syrup for a liquid sweetener. Be sure to buy 100 percent organic pure maple syrup when possible.

stevia

Stevia is a naturally sweet herb that comes in a powder form and a liquid concentrate, and can be 100 to 300 times sweeter than sugar. It has an unusual licorice-like taste that my taste buds can spot from a mile away. Its flavor is intense. I never use it personally, but many who are sugar-phobic love it. Start with a little to see if you like it, and do some experimenting to find the right amount to put in baked goods.

xylitol

This is an alternative sweetener made from birch bark that can be a good substitute for granulated sugar. It's very sweet, so you'll want to use less of it than you would of other sweeteners, which is good, because it's fairly expensive.

spring

zucchini bread

If you've never tried barley flour mixed with brown rice flour, you are in for a treat. Brown rice flour gives a whole new texture to baked goods, crumbly and soft on the inside and a touch crispy on the outside. I love it!

Oil, for pan
1 cup barley flour
½ cup brown rice flour
½ tablespoon baking soda
1 teaspoon baking powder
1 teaspoon cinnamon
¼ teaspoon sea salt
½ cup coconut palm sugar
2 tablespoons flax meal mixed with ⅓ cup applesauce
¼ cup safflower oil
1 teaspoon vanilla flavoring
1 medium zucchini, grated
½ cup chopped nuts (optional)

Preheat oven to 350 degrees F. Spray loaf pan lightly with oil. In a medium bowl, mix together all the dry ingredients except nuts until well combined. In a small bowl, whisk together all wet ingredients until well combined. Pour wet ingredients into dry ingredients and stir until well combined and no lumps remain. Stir in nuts, if using. Pour batter into loaf pan and smooth over the top. Bake for 45 minutes, or until a toothpick inserted in the center comes out clean.

---

springtime lemon bars

Lemon bars are usually filled with refined sugar and other not-so-good-for-you stuff. My healthy version has a delicious raw crust made from dates and almonds. Agar-agar gives the topping a firm texture without eggs.

10 dates, soaked 1 hour, then pitted
2 cups raw sliced almonds, washed
½ cup raw shredded coconut (optional)
2 tablespoons agar-agar
1 cup apple juice
3 tablespoons arrowroot, dissolved in ⅓ cup date soaking water
1 cup rice milk
1 lemon, zested and juiced

¼ cup coconut palm sugar
2 teaspoons lemon extract
2 tablespoons coconut flour or flakes (optional), for topping

Take dates out of water but save date soaking water to use later. Blend almonds and pitted dates along with coconut, if using, in food processor until well mixed, about four minutes. Be sure to scrape down the edges of the bowl to incorporate all the ingredients. Press evenly into an 8x8 glass dish or into a casserole dish to make crust. Refrigerate while you make the topping.

For the topping, combine agar-agar and apple juice in a small saucepan. Bring to a boil, then simmer until all the agar-agar has dissolved and no clear bits remain. Stir occasionally. This could take 10 to 15 minutes. It's very important that the agar-agar is dissolved completely. Meanwhile, mix your arrowroot and date soaking water together until well dissolved. Pour into saucepan with all the remaining ingredients except coconut flour and bring back to a boil. Simmer for five minutes, until sauce becomes thick and creamy. Pour evenly over crust and let cool to room temperature before storing in fridge for 30 minutes. Spread coconut flour or flakes evenly over the top. Cut into squares and serve.

lemon amasake custard

 • Makes 2 to 3 servings

I love lemon so much I could eat this dessert every day. So healthy, yet so tasty, amasake makes the perfect base for pudding or custard. Great with granola.

1 carton (16 ounces) Amazake, plain flavor
½ cup brown rice or maple syrup
1 lemon, zested and juiced (save some zest for garnish)
1 teaspoon vanilla flavoring
3 tablespoons arrowroot, dissolved in ½ cup apple juice
Mint leaves, for garnish

Place all ingredients except diluted arrowroot in small saucepan. Bring to boil and simmer for two minutes to incorporate all the ingredients. Stir in diluted arrowroot and bring back to a boil. Simmer while stirring for a few minutes, until custard thickens. Transfer to a bowl and allow to cool to room temperature before putting in the fridge to cool completely. Serve chilled in bowls garnished with lemon zest and mint. You can serve with sliced strawberries or other fruit.

blissful definition

Amazake is a commonly found brand of amasake, which can be found at any natural food store in the refrigerated section.

lemon meringue cupcakes with lemon coconut frosting • 217

lemon meringue cupcakes with lemon coconut frosting

 • Makes 12 cupcakes

These are fantastic on their own, or you can throw in some fresh blueberries or cranberries. The frosting has no refined sugar, like most frostings made with powdered sugar, and is delicious!

2 tablespoons oil, plus more for pan
1 cup all-purpose flour
1 cup kamut flour (or other whole-grain flour like spelt)
1 cup coconut palm sugar
½ teaspoon baking soda
1 teaspoon baking powder
¼ teaspoon sea salt
2 tablespoons lemon zest (plus more for garnish)
¼ cup lemon juice (about 2 small lemons)
1 cup unsweetened rice or almond milk
1 tablespoon apple cider vinegar
1 teaspoon vanilla flavoring
1 teaspoon lemon extract (optional), for more lemon flavor

lemon coconut frosting

makes about 2½ cups

1 package Mori Nu silken tofu
½ cup maple syrup
1 tablespoon vanilla flavoring
1 teaspoon lemon extract
2 tablespoon lemon juice
2 tablespoons arrowroot
⅓ cup coconut palm sugar
½ cup coconut oil, melted

Preheat oven to 350 degrees F. Spray muffin tin with oil or line with cupcake liners. Mix together dry ingredients in a large bowl. In separate bowl, whisk together wet ingredients. Add wet ingredients to dry ingredients and mix until well combined. Spoon into muffin tin until almost full. Bake for 20 minutes, or until toothpick inserted in the center comes out clean.

While cupcakes are baking make your frosting. Combine all ingredients except the coconut oil into a food processor. Blend until well combined. Be sure to scrape down the edges of the bowl a few times to incorporate all the ingredients. With the blade running, slowly drizzle in the coconut oil. Refrigerate frosting for 20 minutes before icing cupcakes. When cupcakes are cool, top with frosting then garnish with lemon zest.

blissful variation

This cupcake recipe can be used as a base to make any flavor cupcake you would like. For example, sub the lemon for orange (also in the frosting) and add fresh raspberries to the cupcake base. Or remove lemon and add 1 cup cocoa powder and ½ cup chocolate chips to cupcake base, and sub lemon for melted chocolate in the frosting. The possibilities are endless!

summer

blueberry-hemp drops

 • Makes about 25 balls

This is the best treat if you want something chocolaty and tart that's guilt-free. It also makes the best snack before or after a workout. The sesame seeds add calcium and the hemp protein adds omegas.

1 cup dried unsweetened blueberries
1 cup dried unsweetened cranberries
½ cup raw walnuts
¼ cup raw sunflower seeds
1 tablespoon sesame seeds
½ cup dried shredded coconut, plus ½ cup for rolling
¼ cup hemp protein powder
¼ cup maple syrup
¼ cup raw cacao powder (optional)
¼ cup vegan grain-sweetened chocolate chips (optional)

Place dried fruit and nuts in a food processor and blend for about one minute. Pour in the rest of the ingredients, except chocolate chips, if using, and process until no chunks remain, about 20 seconds. Toss in chocolate chips if using and pulse for 10 seconds to combine.

With wet fingers, scoop out one tablespoon-sized portion of mixture, roll into a ball, then roll in shredded coconut. Place on a plate and continue until all the mixture is gone. Refrigerate for 30 minutes to firm up the balls. Store in an airtight container in the fridge for up to a week.

---

ginger cookies

S 45 • Makes about one dozen 2-inch cookies

This may be a bit doughier and less crispy than the ginger snaps you are used to, but they're much healthier. If you want a spicier cookie, feel free to add more ginger.

½ cup kamut or spelt flour
¼ cup brown rice flour
1 teaspoon ground ginger
Dash cinnamon
Dash nutmeg
⅛ teaspoon sea salt
2 tablespoons arrowroot
1 tablespoon flax meal mixed with 3 tablespoons applesauce
⅓ cup maple syrup
2 tablespoons coconut palm sugar

blueberry-hemp drops • 218

2 tablespoons safflower oil
½ teaspoon vanilla flavoring

Preheat oven to 325 degrees F. Line a cookie sheet with parchment paper. Whisk together the first seven ingredients in a medium bowl. In a smaller bowl, whisk together the rest of the ingredients until well combined. Fold wet ingredients into dry ingredients and mix until well combined.

Spray a rounded tablespoon or ice cream scooper with oil and use to drop rounds of batter onto the cookie sheet, about two inches apart. Bake for 12 minutes. Pull out and lightly flatten cookie dough with the bottom of a cup. Bake another 8 to 10 minutes. Allow to rest for one minute, then transfer to a cooling rack. Can be stored in an airtight container for up to three days.

blissful suggestion

These are great layered with bananas and *peanut butter-like mousse* (recipe follows).

peanut butter-like mousse

G 45 • Makes 4 to 6 servings

I use soy nut butter in this recipe instead of peanut butter, but you are welcome to use whichever you prefer. In fact, you could probably use any nut butter you want for this recipe.

2 packages Mori Nu silken tofu
¾ cup unsweetened creamy soy nut butter
⅓ cup coconut palm sugar
⅔ cup maple syrup
1 tablespoon arrowroot
2 teaspoons vanilla flavoring
Pinch sea salt

Combine all ingredients in a food processor and blend until well combined. Be sure to scrape the edges of the bowl a few times to incorporate all the ingredients. Chill in the fridge for 20 minutes to stiffen.

heavenly raw chocolate mousse

G S 45 • Makes 2 to 3 servings • FAN FAVE

This is a chocolaty dessert that you don't have to feel guilty for eating! Avocados make the base for this mousse instead of heart-clogging butter, cream, and eggs. I use raw cacao, which is chocolate in its natural, unprocessed state.

2 ripe avocados
12 dates, soaked for 2 hours and pitted, or ¾ cup maple syrup
⅓ cup raw cacao powder
1 teaspoon vanilla flavoring or 1 fresh vanilla bean
4 strawberries, sliced

Blend dates in a food processor until they become a paste. Add all the rest of the ingredients except the berries and blend until smooth. Be sure to scrape the edges of the bowl a few times to incorporate everything.

Serve in a martini glass with sliced strawberries on top.

peanut butter-like mousse • 220
ginger cookies • 218

fan ★ fave

heavenly raw chocolate mousse • 220

blissful definition

Raw *cacao* comes from a tropical evergreen tree. The seed is ground into a powder that has many antioxidants and minerals. It's great to make a hot chocolate with or put in smoothies.

---

strawberry-mint limeade

   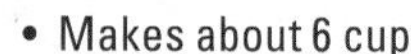 • Makes about 6 cups

Not quite a dessert, but I wanted to include this delicious drink somewhere! I made this for a Fourth of July party, and it was a big hit. It's the perfect summertime beverage to have by the pool, too.

2 cups fresh strawberries, tops removed and sliced in half
2 tablespoons lime zest
¼ cup lime juice (about 3 to 4 limes)
3 tablespoons mint, chopped
⅓ cup maple syrup
1 cup filtered water
2 cups ice, or more for desired texture
Mint leaves, for garnish

Blend all ingredients except mint leaves in a blender until smooth and no chunks remain. Serve cold, garnished with mint leaves.

strawberry-mint limeade • 222

coconut-orange bread pudding • 225

autumn

coconut-chocolate bars

S • Makes 12 bars

Not to toot my own horn here, but these are deliciously decadent. Coconut and chocolate is a match made in heaven, and this bar will get you through the toughest of chocolate cravings. They take quite a bit of time to set, so don't make these if you need a dessert in a hurry.

Oil, for dish
1¾ cups barley flour (or other whole-grain flour)
½ teaspoon baking powder
1 tablespoon vanilla flavoring
½ cup coconut oil, melted
¼ teaspoon sea salt
1 cup vegan grain-sweetened chocolate chips
7 ounces coconut milk
3 tablespoons maple syrup
Grated dried coconut and sliced almonds

Preheat oven to 350 degrees F. Coat a 9x9 baking dish with oil spray, then line it with parchment paper. Spray again. This will allow for easy removal of the bars. Stir together the next five ingredients in a medium bowl until well combined. Press into bottom of prepared pan and bake for 25 minutes or until golden. Set aside.

Meanwhile, place chocolate chips in a medium saucepan and heat over low flame. Whisk in the coconut milk and maple syrup. After chocolate mixture is smooth, remove from heat and pour over prepared crust. Sprinkle with coconut and almonds and leave to cool. Once cool, put in refrigerator for five hours or more.

---

coconut-orange bread pudding

S 45 • Makes 8 to 10 servings

I never really liked bread pudding until I went vegan. It's a comforting dessert, and I like mine with a touch of orange and coconut.

1 pound bread (whole wheat or other whole grain), cubed
1 cup raisins
1 can (13½ ounce) coconut milk
1 cup almond milk
1 teaspoon orange extract
1 cup coconut palm sugar
1 orange, zested and juiced
2 tablespoons arrowroot, dissolved in orange juice

Place bread and raisins in a 9x13 baking dish. Preheat oven to 350 degrees F. In a small saucepan whisk together the coconut milk, almond milk, extract, and sugar over a low flame. In a small bowl whisk together the orange zest, juice, and arrowroot until well dissolved. Pour into saucepan with other ingredients and whisk over medium flame until sauce begins to thicken, about five minutes. Pour over bread, mix until all the bread is covered, and press evenly into the dish. Bake covered for 25 minutes.

---

gluten-free peanut butter cookies

G S 45 • Makes about 1½ dozen cookies • **CHEF FAVE**

This is the only recipe you'll find in this cookbook that uses vegan margarine and egg replacer. These two baking substitutes help create a super rich cookie and help bind the gluten-free flours together. It's almost sinful. Feel free to cut this recipe in half for a smaller batch.

¼ cup vegan margarine or coconut oil, melted
½ cup maple syrup
⅓ cup unsweetened applesauce
1 teaspoon Ener-G egg replacer, whisked with 1 tablespoon water
1 teaspoon vanilla flavoring
½ cup peanut butter
¾ cup almond flour
¾ cup brown rice flour
1 teaspoon baking powder
1 teaspoon baking soda
2 teaspoons flax meal
¼ teaspoon sea salt
1 teaspoon arrowroot
½ cup vegan grain-sweetened chocolate chips (optional)

Preheat oven to 350 degrees F. Line two cookie sheets with parchment paper. In medium mixing bowl, beat margarine, maple syrup, and applesauce until smooth and creamy. Add the rest of wet ingredients and mix well. In separate bowl, whisk together flours, baking powder and soda, flax, salt, and arrowroot. Mix wet into dry ingredients until well combined. Fold in chocolate chips and stir well.

Drop spoonfuls onto prepared cookie sheet. Using wet fingertips or the bottom of a glass, press down each cookie evenly (continue to dip fingers or glass in water to prevent sticking). The cookies will not spread much, so you can put them close together on the cookie sheet. Take a fork and press lightly on the top in two directions, to create a grid on top of the cookie. Bake for 18 to 20 minutes, or until lightly browned. Remove from oven and cool cookies on a wire rack.

---

gluten-free chocolate chip cookies

G S 45 • Makes about 2 dozen cookies

Many gluten-free cookies tend to be dry, but these have a nice rich taste and texture without much oil. These are a big hit for my clients looking for a healthy, tasty, gluten-free treat. Depending on how long your flour has been sitting out, the mixture may be too wet and you may need to add a touch more flour. You want the dough to be solid and not sticking all over your hands.

1 cup almond flour
2 cups brown rice flour
½ teaspoon sea salt
½ teaspoon baking soda

chef ★ fave

gluten-free peanut butter cookies • 226

½ teaspoon cinnamon (optional)
1 tablespoon vanilla flavoring
¼ cup safflower oil
¼ cup unsweetened applesauce
½ cup coconut palm sugar
1 tablespoon flax meal, whisked together with 3 tablespoons water
½ cup grain-sweetened chocolate chips

Combine the first four ingredients plus cinnamon, if using, in a medium bowl. Whisk together the remaining ingredients, except chocolate chips, in a small bowl until well combined. Mix wet ingredients into dry ingredients. Fold in chocolate chips. The batter may seem dry, so use your hands to make sure the dough is well mixed. Let sit in the refrigerator for 20 minutes. Preheat oven to 350 degrees F.

Place one-inch balls of dough on a parchment-lined baking sheet about two inches apart from each other. Wet the bottom of a glass and press down the balls of dough gently, or use wet fingertips. Bake about 10 minutes, until tops are golden brown. Let cool for a few minutes, then transfer to a cooling rack.

---

pear pie with homemade flaky crust

S • Makes 6 to 8 servings

You'll find that this is the easiest pie crust to make, with a nice delicate crumb. You can use whatever fruit is in season, so enjoy it year-round!

pear pie filling

4 D'Anjou pears (or any fruit), cored and sliced
½ cup raisins
1 cup apple juice
Dash cinnamon
Dash nutmeg
Pinch sea salt
1 tablespoon arrowroot, dissolved in 3 tablespoons water

flaky pie crust

3 cups whole-wheat pastry flour
½ teaspoon sea salt
½ cup plus 2 tablespoons oil
½ cup water

Place all filling ingredients but arrowroot in small saucepan. Bring to boil and simmer, covered, for 10 minutes or until pears are cooked. Turn off flame. Dissolve arrowroot in water and stir until no lumps remain. Stir arrowroot into pears until well coated.

Preheat the oven to 350 degrees F. Meanwhile, make the pie crust by placing the flour and salt in a medium bowl. Slowly add in the oil while stirring with a fork. You should get little beads of flour. Stir in water and knead with hands until the dough forms a ball. Roll out on parchment paper in a thin circle about two inches thick and 10 inches in diameter. Place pie pan on top of dough and gracefully flip dough and parchment over. Remove parchment and press dough into pie pan. Prick dough a few times with a fork and bake for 15 minutes. Remove and set aside.

Pour pear mixture into pie pan and use the leftover dough to make a lattice or another design on top. Bake for 15 minutes.

blissful suggestion

This is great topped with *lemon crème sauce*, on page 36. Feel free to use this crust for any pie or quiche recipe.

blissful living: show gratitude

When you sit down for lunch or dinner, show gratitude for the meal you are about to eat. Show appreciation for the many people that took part in getting that food to your plate: the person who planted the seeds, drove the produce to the store, and the person who stocked the shelf. Even give thanks to those who crafted the chopsticks or silverware, and the plate you are eating on!

winter

pear-almond coffee cake

S • Makes 9 servings

I haven't had coffee cake in ages because it's typically full of oil and sugar. So I chose to make my own with coconut oil and applesauce to reduce the oil greatly. This makes the cake so moist and delicious! You could try to go sans oil in the cake part and add more applesauce.

topping

¾ cup barley flour
½ cup coconut palm sugar
2 tablespoons coconut oil, melted
1 teaspoon lemon juice
1 teaspoon cinnamon
1 cup pear, small cubes

cake

1 cup barley flour
½ cup brown rice flour
1 teaspoon baking powder
1 tablespoon flax meal
½ teaspoon sea salt
½ teaspoon cinnamon
¼ cup coconut oil, melted
¾ cup coconut palm sugar
½ cup applesauce
2 teaspoons almond extract
½ cup rice milk mixed with 2 teaspoons apple cider vinegar

Prepare topping by mixing together all the ingredients, except pear, until well combined (I like to use my hands for this). The texture will be crumbly and dry. Stir in pear and set aside.

Preheat oven to 350 degrees F. For the cake, whisk together first six ingredients in a medium bowl. In another bowl whisk together the coconut oil and sugar. Stir in the rest of the wet ingredients until well combined. Fold in wet to dry ingredients and mix until well combined. Pour in lightly oiled 8x8 baking dish (or similar size). Sprinkle topping mixture evenly over the top of the cake and gently press in. Bake uncovered for one hour. Test with a toothpick and if it comes out clean the cake is done.

---

ginger rice pudding

G S 45 • Makes 4 to 6 servings

This is a healthy yet tasty dessert that is great on a cold night. Ginger is great for warming you up, and when paired with coconut, it makes a rich, soothing treat.

1 cup long-grain brown rice, washed
Pinch sea salt
2½ cups filtered water
1 can (13½ ounces) light coconut milk

pear-almond coffee cake • 230

1 tablespoon fresh ginger, minced
¼ cup maple syrup, or more to taste
⅓ cup raisins
Dash cinnamon
Shredded coconut, for garnish

pressure cooking method

Place all ingredients except cinnamon in a pressure cooker. Lock lid and bring to pressure over medium flame. When up to pressure, cook for 30 to 40 minutes. Turn off flame, let it come down from pressure, open, and stir in cinnamon. Garnish with coconut.

boiling method

Place all ingredients except cinnamon in a medium pot and bring to a boil. Simmer, covered, for 30 to 40 minutes, or until rice is cooked but not dried out. Stir in cinnamon. Garnish with coconut.

blissful suggestion

For a special treat layer rice pudding in a cup with *velvety chocolate mousse*, on page 236, to make a rice pudding chocolate parfait.

pumpkin hot chocolate • 233

no-oil pumpkin spice bread

• Makes 9 servings

You will not believe that this dessert has no oil! It's so rich, delicious, and moist that you would never guess that it's good for you. The chocolate chips are optional, but I think they are perfectly paired with the pumpkin flavors of this holiday time bread.

Oil, for baking dish
1 cup brown rice flour
1¼ cup barley flour (spelt or other whole-grain flour is fine)
1 teaspoon baking powder
1 teaspoon baking soda
½ teaspoon sea salt
2 teaspoons pumpkin spice mix
1½ cup coconut palm sugar
3 tablespoons unsweetened plain soy yogurt
1 can (15 ounces) pumpkin
¼ cup unsweetened applesauce
2 teaspoons vanilla flavoring
½ cup vegan grain-sweetened chocolate chips

Preheat oven to 350 degrees F. Whisk together first six dry ingredients in a medium bowl. In another bowl whisk together the rest of the ingredients except chocolate chips. Fold in wet to dry ingredients and mix until well combined. If using chocolate chips fold them into the batter. Pour into lightly oiled 8x8 baking dish and smooth over the top. Bake for 60 minutes. Test with a toothpick and if it comes out clean the bread is done.

blissful variation

For *no-oil banana bread*, substitute about 2 cups mashed bananas for the pumpkin and 1 teaspoon cinnamon for the pumpkin pie spice.

---

pumpkin hot chocolate

G S 45 • Makes 2 servings

I always find that I have leftover pumpkin after Thanksgiving or Christmas dinner. The perfect way to use up that pumpkin is to make this sweet and warming drink.

½ can (15 ounces) pumpkin, or ½ cup pumpkin puree (page 43)
3 to 4 tablespoons unsweetened cocoa powder
Dash cinnamon
Dash nutmeg
1 teaspoon vanilla flavoring
2 cups vanilla soy milk or rice milk
2 tablespoon maple syrup, or more to taste

Combine first five ingredients in a medium saucepan. Slowly whisk in milk over medium flame, until all ingredients are well incorporated. Whisk in maple syrup. Do not boil.

anytime

chewy trail mix bars

S 45 • Makes about 12 to 15 bars

We all know that refined sugar is not good for us, makes us feel sluggish, and has negative effects on our mood and health. Give these chewy trail mix bars a try, which have almonds for added protein.

2 cups brown rice crispy cereal (unsweetened preferred)
2 cups rolled oats
1 cup raisins or other dried fruit
⅓ cup sesame seeds
½ cup pecans, chopped
½ cup almonds, chopped
1½ cups brown rice syrup
1 cup almond butter
1 teaspoon vanilla flavoring

Mix dry ingredients in a large bowl. Set aside. Heat last three ingredients over low flame until well incorporated, about five minutes. Pour over dry ingredients and use your hand or a stiff spatula to mix until all ingredients are coated with wet mixture.

Line a 9x13 casserole dish with parchment paper or lightly oil. Press mixture into dish evenly with parchment paper or wet hands to keep it from sticking to your hands. Set aside to cool, about one hour. Then cut to desired size. This will keep in an airtight container for a week.

orange-kissed almond macaroons

G S 45 • Makes about 20 pieces

I never liked dried coconut until about three years ago because I thought the texture was funny. Then one day I realized I liked it! These macaroons have a touch of orange zest and almond extract to create a new spin on the traditional macaroon. Sweetened with brown rice syrup or coconut nectar, this treat will leave you feeling guilt-free!

3 cups dried unsweetened coconut
½ cup sliced almonds
⅓ cup brown rice flour
½ cup nondairy milk mixed with 2 tablespoons flax meal
1 cup brown rice syrup or coconut nectar
2 tablespoons coconut oil, melted
1 orange, zested
1 teaspoon almond extract
1 recipe *chocolate ganache sauce*, on page 235

Preheat oven to 325 degrees F. Lightly toast coconut in a dry skillet, stirring continuously, until golden color. Combine with all ingredients in a large bowl and stir until everything is well incorporated. With wet hands, form into small balls and place on

chewy trail mix bars • 234

parchment-lined cookie sheet (I keep a small bowl of water nearby for wetting my hands, which prevents the dough from sticking). Continue until all the dough is gone. Place in oven and bake for 15 to 20 minutes.

Meanwhile, make your ganache topping, if using.

Remove macaroons from oven and allow them to cool completely. Place on a plate, then put in the refrigerator for 15 minutes. Dip each one into the chocolate by holding the bottom and rolling it around to almost get the bottom of the macaroon. Place back on plate and allow to cool. Store in fridge for one hour to make sure the chocolate hardens.

chocolate ganache sauce

S 45 • Makes about 1 cup

1 cup grain-sweetened chocolate chips
½ cup rice milk (soy or almond is fine)

Melt down the chocolate chips in a small saucepan over a low flame with milk, stirring continuously.

velvety chocolate mousse with berry sauce and toasted walnuts

G ◊ 45 • Makes 3 to 5 servings

This rich, creamy, chocolaty treat will make everyone happy! The berry sauce is great when strawberries are at their peak during the summer months, but you can have the mousse year-round.

2 packages Mori Nu silken tofu
¾ cup maple syrup
2 teaspoons vanilla flavoring
½ cup vegan grain-sweetened chocolate chips, melted down
⅓ cup cocoa powder

berry sauce

2 cups mixed berries
¾ cup apple juice
1 tablespoon brown rice syrup or maple syrup
1 tablespoon lemon juice
Pinch cinnamon
½ cup walnuts, toasted and chopped, for garnish

In a food processor, blend the mousse ingredients until mixed well. Be sure to scrape down edges with a spatula a few times. Refrigerate for one hour.

Place berries and apple juice in medium saucepan and heat over low flame, until berries begin to break apart, stirring occasionally. Add remaining ingredients, except nuts, and stir well. Allow to cool. Pour mousse into individual cups; top with berry sauce and walnuts.

wheat-free fudgy chocolate brownies

◊ • Makes 9 to 12 brownies

Even though these have very little oil, they are not the least bit cakey or dry. Great on their own, paired with chocolate ganache *on page 235, or made into a brownie sundae with coconut ice cream. Honestly, that is the way I prefer it!*

Oil, for dish
1 package Mori Nu silken tofu
⅓ cup maple syrup
1½ cups coconut palm sugar
½ cup unsweetened cocoa powder
⅓ cup applesauce
2 tablespoons safflower oil
2 tablespoons vanilla flavoring
1¼ cups barley flour
½ teaspoon baking powder
Pinch sea salt
Pinch cinnamon
½ cup grain-sweetened chocolate chips

Preheat oven to 350 degrees F. In a food processor, blend the first seven ingredients until smooth, making sure to scrape around the bowl a few times to incorporate all ingredients. Place remaining ingredients, except chocolate chips, in a medium bowl and mix in the wet ingredients. Stir until well combined, then fold in chocolate chips.

Spray an 8x8 baking dish with oil spray and pour batter into dish, smoothing batter evenly. Bake for 40 to 50 minutes; insert toothpick into the center to test if done. Let cool and serve.

"One cannot think well, love well, sleep well, if one has not dined well."

— Virginia Woolf

more

I wanted this book to be more than just a cookbook and serve as a guide in your journey to bliss. In this section you will find sample menus in case all of these recipes alone seem daunting, and some plant-based resources that can help answer any questions you may have. If those resources do not help, feel free to contact me via my website, theblissfulchef.com.

more

sample menus

To help you on the quest for seasonal eating and balance in your diet, I've included some sample menus for each season. Since the recipes are listed by season, it is easy to pick and choose a meal, but the list below is made up of recipes I like to serve together. Included are menu ideas for other popular occasions, as well as meals that kids love.

spring

breakfast

coconut bliss granola with key-lime soy yogurt (page 35)

lunch

love your heart beet soup (page 63)
spring kale salad with sweet miso dressing (page 88)
blackened tempeh caesar wrap (page 182)

dinner

black-eyed pea bbq stew (page 182)
lemon-roasted asparagus (page 112)
brown rice (page 160)
orange-wakame cucumber salad (page 172)

dessert

springtime lemon bars (page 214)

summer

breakfast

sweet polenta porridge (page 41)
or strawberry shortcake smoothie (page 41)

lunch

chilled corn bisque (page 66)
curry chicken-less salad wrap (page 187)

dinner

penne with creamy red pepper sauce (page 145)
steamed broccoli (page 107)

dessert

heavenly raw chocolate mousse (page 220)

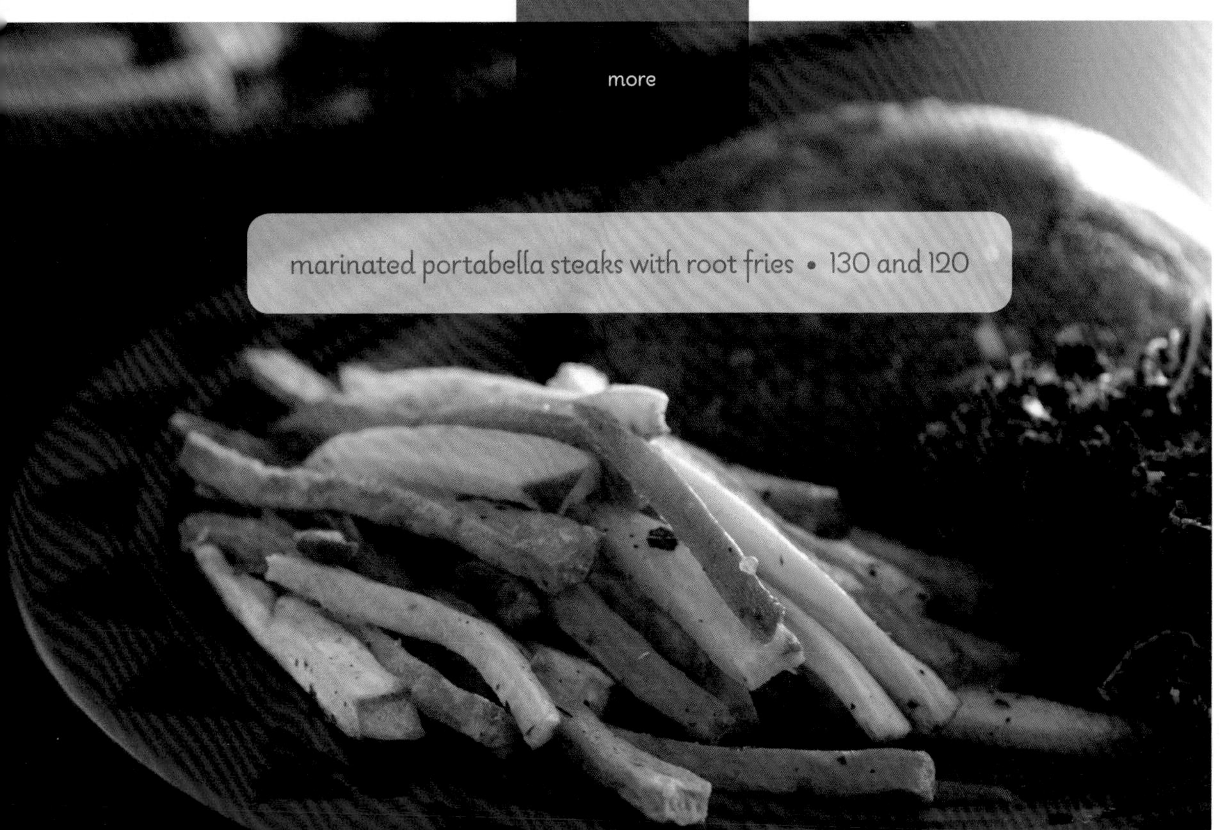

marinated portabella steaks with root fries • 130 and 120

autumn

breakfast
thyme for miso (page 74) with steamed greens

lunch
tempeh avocado sushi rolls (page 162)
fried kabocha with peanut sauce (page 82)

dinner
millet mashed "potatoes" (page 149)
blanched greens with basil-pecan pesto sauce (page 129)
maple-glazed tempeh (page 195)

dessert
coconut-orange bread pudding (page 225)

winter

breakfast
gluten-free savory biscuits with apricot-blueberry fruit compote (page 49)

lunch
millet-black bean burgers (page 198)
blanched greens (page 107)

dinner
marinated portabella steaks (page 130)
not-so-forbidden rice salad (page 155)
perfect winter stew (page 126)

dessert
wheat-free fudgy chocolate brownie sundae (page 236)

bbq and picnic food

mango-pineapple tropical soup (page 69)
marinated portabella steaks (page 130)
not-your-average cabbage slaw (page 100)
barbecued seitan burger (page 192)
un-tuna salad (page 206)
southwest grilled corn salad (page 117)
hawaiian tofu and veggie kabobs (page 187)
strawberry-mint limeade (page 222)

lunch on the go

blackened tempeh caesar wrap (page 182) with wasabi sweet potato salad (page 116)
land and sea soba salad with steamed greens (page 169)
curry chicken-less salad wrap (page 187) with mac n' kale salad (page 100)
macrobiotic lunch – brown rice (page 160), basic beans (page 202), steamed greens, orange-wakame cucumber salad (page 172)

perfect no-oil potluck dishes

spring
spring kale salad with sweet miso dressing (page 88)
blanched greens with basil-pecan pesto sauce (page 129)
spring green casserole (page 113)
barley "hato mugi" pilaf (page 141)
simple lemon-scented basmati rice (page 143)

summer
fresh green salad with cilantro-lime dressing (page 93)
nishime (page 117)
asian millet and quinoa pilaf (page 149)
fiesta quinoa salad (page 147)
red quinoa salad (page 145)

autumn
pumpkin with apricot glaze (page 119)
sweet potato puree (page 122)

winter
gingery bok choy-burdock sauté (page 125)
miso-baked daikon (page 126)
not-so-forbidden rice salad (page 155)

food for the kiddos

strawberry shortcake smoothie (page 41)
mixed berry couscous surprise (page 39)
tofu scramble sammich (page 52)
tofu salad (eggless egg salad) wrap (page 188)
penne with creamy red pepper (page 145)
macro "mac and cheeze" (page 150)
pan-fried tofu with carrot-ginger sauce (page 198)
chewy trail mix bars (page 234)

resources

Most of the ingredients used in this cookbook should be available at your local natural food store. If you can't find a particular product locally, you can try these resources below. I've noted the city where they're based along with the phone number and website. You can also replace a hard-to-find ingredient with something similar. Feel free to e-mail me at info@theblissfulchef.com if you have specific questions about substituting ingredients in a recipe.

macrobiotic products

Eden Foods
Clinton, Michigan
888-424-EDEN (3336)
www.edenfoods.com

Gold Mine Natural Food Company
San Diego, California
858-537-9830
www.goldminenaturalfoods.com

Maine Coast Sea Vegetables
Franklin, Maine
207-565-2907
www.seaveg.com

Mitoku
Natural Import Company
Biltmore Village, North Carolina
800-324-1878
www.naturalimport.com

Simply Natural/Discount Natural Foods
Hooksett, New Hampshire
888-392-9237
www.simply-natural.biz

other vegan and raw/living products and clothing

Alternative Outfitters (clothing, shoes, gifts, and accessories)
Pasadena, California
866-758-5837
www.alternativeoutfitters.com

Bob's Red Mill Natural Foods (grains, beans, flours, gluten-free products, and baking supplies)
Milwaukie, Oregon 97222
800-349-2173
www.bobsredmill.com

Cosmo's Vegan Shoppe (vegan products, food items, books, body care, and accessories)
Marietta, Georgia
800-260-9968
www.cosmosveganshoppe.com

Herbivore Clothing (clothing, shoes, gifts, and accessories)
Portland, Oregon
503-281-TOFU (8638)
www.herbivoreclothing.com

Pangea Vegan Store (vegan products, food items, body care, clothing, and accessories)
Rockville, Maryland
800-340-1200
www.veganstore.com

Ultimate Superfoods (raw/living food and products)
800-728-2066
www.ultimatesuperfoods.com

The Vegan Collection (clothing, gifts, shoes, and accessories)
Los Angeles, California
626-722-8340
www.thevegancollection.com

Vegan Essentials (vegan products, food items, books, body care, and accessories)
Waukesha, Wisconsin
866-88-VEGAN (83426)
www.veganessentials.com

recommended reading and viewing

I completely endorse the books and DVDs below. When switching to a plant-based diet, it's important to have resources that are accurate, informative, educational, and transformational. These selections have influenced the way I eat and feel about food, and some have even shown me how my choices affect more than my physical self. I hope you will enjoy them.

macrobiotic and healing books

Food and Healing, by Anne Marie Colbin
Hip Chick's Guide to Macrobiotics, by Jessica Porter
The Kind Diet, by Alicia Silverstone
Love, Sanae, by Sanae Suzuki
The Macrobiotic Way, by Michio Kushi
Staying Healthy With the Seasons, by Dr. Elson M. Haas
Sugar Blues, by William Dufty

health and nutrition books

Becoming Vegan, by Brenda Davis and Vesanto Melina
Breaking the Food Seduction, by Dr. Neal Barnard
The China Study, by T. Colin Campbell
Diet for a New America, by John Robbins
Eat to Live, by Dr. Joel Fuhrman
The Engine 2 Diet, by Rip Esselstyn
The Thrive Diet, by Brendan Brasier

ethical/spiritual books

Eating Animals, by Jonathan Safran Foer
Mad Cowboy, by Howard F. Lyman
The New Good Life, by John Robbins
The Omnivore's Dilemma, by Michael Pollan
Thanking the Monkey, by Karen Dawn
Vegan: The New Ethics of Eating, by Erik Marcus
The World Peace Diet, by Will Tuttle
Why We Love Dogs, Eat Pigs, and Wear Cows, by Melanie Joy

dvds

Earthlings, by Shaun Monson
Food Inc., by Robert Kenner
Forks Over Knives, by Lee Fulkerson
Future of Food, by Deborah Koons Garcia
Simply Raw: Reversing Diabetes in 30 Days

places to study

As the plant-based diet grows in popularity, there are more and more schools, conferences, and online programs where you can learn more. If you want to make healthy eating your next career or want to learn the ins and outs of plant-based culinary techniques, these places to study can give you a wealth of knowledge. Some have master's programs; many have shorter programs and online programs to fit everyone's budget and schedule.

Bastyr University
Kenmore, Washington
(425) 823-1300
www.bastyr.edu

Bauman College
Santa Cruz, California, and Boulder, Colorado
800-987-7530
www.baumancollege.org
Online programs available

French Meadows Macrobiotic
Summer Camp
Tahoe National Forest, California
800-232-2372
www.ohsawamacrobiotics.com

Institute for Integrative Nutrition
New York City, New York
877-730-5444
www.integrativenutrition.com
Online programs available

Kushi Institute
Becket, Maine
800-975-8744
www.kushiinstitute.org

Macrobiotics America with David and Cynthia Biscoe
Oroville, California
530-532-1918
www.macroamerica.com
Online programs available

The Natural Epicurean Academy of Culinary Arts
Austin, Texas
512-476-2276
www.naturalepicurean.com

The Natural Gourmet Institute
New York, New York
212-645-5170
www.naturalgourmetinstitute.com

The Christina Pirello School of Natural Cooking and Integrative Health Studies
Philadelphia, Pennsylvania
800-939-3909
www.christinacooks.com

Strengthening Health Institute
Philadelphia, Pennsylvania
215-238-9212
www.strengthenhealth.org

T. Colin Campbell Foundation
Certificate in Plant-based Nutrition
866-326-7635
www.ecornell.com/l-PBN
Online program only

favorite online resources

www.christinacooks.com
www.pcrm.org
www.thehealthyhipchick.com
www.healingcuisine.com
www.healthyvoyager.com
www.macrobiotics.co.uk
www.ohsawamacrobiotics.com
www.supervegan.com
www.vegan.com
www.vegetariantimes.com
www.vegweb.com

To see a list of my favorite blogs, including some by my food testers, visit my Blogroll on my personal blog at *www.theblissfulchef.com.*

acknowledgments

I would like to extend my thanks and gratitude to the following people:

My editor, Debbie Harmsen, and her assistant, Sara, at BenBella Books for all their patience and hard work put in with the editing of my first book. My publisher, Glenn Yeffeth at BenBella, for taking a chance on me. My agent, Michael Ebeling, for also taking a chance on me. Kit and the design and production team for designing the most beautiful book of my dreams. My writing coach, Martha Murphy, for helping me discover my ability to write.

My friends, who supported and loved me even when I was a stressed maniac, who nurtured my creative spirit, and allowed me to stuff their faces with experimental food. And to all those who helped during cooking classes, photo shoots, and other events, I could not have done any of this without you.

Thank you to all my teachers, who have helped me grow into a magnificent chef and teacher, who continue to support me and teach me new things—Jessica, Christina, Sanae and Eric, Morgan, Chuck, Sheri, David, Neal, Colin, Verne, Bill, Warren, Will, Melanie, Bob, Meredith, Dawn, Brendan, Brian, Denny, Fran, Bryant, Ani, Julia and Carl, Mary, Rawsheed, Rip, Master Henry, and Rainbeau, to name a few.

To my photographers, Melissa Schwartz (*www.schwartzstudios.com*) and Melanie Shatto (*www.melaniemorganshatto.com*), thanks for creating beauty with my food and sharing so much of your time with me to make this book stunning.

To my lovely recipe testers (noted below), who worked so hard, also stuffing their faces, scouring natural food stores to find ingredients, and experimenting on their friends and family, I owe you a big thanks! You all had such great feedback, were honest about what sucked and what rocked your world, and helped me make the instructions easier to follow!

- Danielle Richardet (*www.itstartswithme-danielle.blogspot.com*) was my all-star tester, happily testing everything I could give her and trying it out on her kiddos.
- Lisa Pitman (*www.veganculinarycrusade.com*)
- Ryan Keck
- Erin Scott (*www.veg-espot.blogspot.com*)
- Judith Barnes (*www.bigrawblog.blogspot.com*)
- Leinana Two Moons (*www.vegangoodthings.blogspot.com*)
- Helen Pitlick (*www.vegtastic.net*)
- Christine Oppenheim (*www.veggiefixation.com*)
- Barrie Allen
- Carrie Underwood
- Meg Claire (*www.yogasavestheday.net*)
- Morgan Anger (*www.littlehouseofveggies.blogspot.com*)
- Christina "La Vegetaliana" Vani (*www.veganinsuburbia.blogspot.com*)
- Stefania Moffatt (*www.ingredientsforlife.ca*)

And lastly, to all my readers and friends in the blogging community. You inspire me each and every day. Thank you for all of your love and support. This book is for you.

about the blissful chef

The Blissful Chef Christy Morgan is a successful vegan macrobiotic chef, whose business is changing people's lives through healthy cooking classes, lectures, personal chef services and private instruction. With her first cookbook *Blissful Bites* and various online and offline articles, she is well-published in the world of natural foods.

But healthful cooking wasn't always Christy's passion. After receiving a degree in fashion design from The University of Texas, she moved to Los Angeles where some vegan friends showed Christy her first PETA video, *Meet Your Meat*, and she instantly converted to a vegan lifestyle. After this, she knew she wanted to help people and have a career that was compassionate, so she moved to Austin and began training at The Natural Epicurean Academy of Culinary Arts.

Culinary school redirected Christy's creativity from fashion to food. After graduating, she moved back to Los Angeles to follow her new dream of helping others make the connection between the mind, body, and spirit, so they may live authentic, healthy, and happy lives. Her fun and informative classes teach amateurs and seasoned veterans alike how to create simple yet delicious, "green" meals using local organic produce and seasonal cooking techniques.

After four years of cooking and teaching in Los Angeles, Christy took to the blogging world, where she shares her knowledge, passion, and delicious recipes with fans around the world.

index

d

m

n

t

u

v

metric conversions

abbreviation key

tsp = teaspoon
tbsp = tablespoon
dsp = dessert spoon

u.s. standard … u.k.

¼ tsp .... ¼ tsp (scant)

½ tsp .... ½ tsp (scant)

¾ tsp .... ½ tsp (rounded)

1 tsp .... ¾ tsp (slightly rounded)

1 tbsp .... 2½ tsp

¼ cup .... ¼ cup minus 1 dsp

⅓ cup .... ¼ cup plus 1 tsp

½ cup .... ⅓ cup plus 2 dsp

⅔ cup .... ½ cup plus 1 tbsp

¾ cup .... ½ cup plus 2 tbsp

1 cup .... ¾ cup and 2 dsp